Praise

'A compelling read for any leader with responsibility for a team, ego can so easily get in the way of authentic leadership. Mary peels back the subject of our ego and how it's formed in a beautifully descriptive way and provides a deep insight for the reader to examine their own challenges with ego, acknowledge it and ditch it!'

— **Craig McMurrough,** Associate Partner, People and Culture Lead, Consulting and Innovation, Capita

'This book takes us on a journey of discovery - about ourselves, our strengths and of course our weaknesses. Never judgemental, it holds a mirror up and teaches us the skills to enable us to identify these for ourselves. Using a "reality check" example in each chapter, we see how real life encounters are matched to the theory, enabling us to gain an understanding of what kind of leaders we truly are. The exercises allow us to signpost potential blindspots and reflect on how these can be managed.'

— **Niall O'Connor**, Group Managing Director, Aldi

'A wonderfully useful whistle-stop tour to help "you" get out of the way of your ability to lead. Options you can play with to ensure you distinguish between your ego and your vision. Highly recommended to anyone getting frustrated with others in trying to achieve their goals.'

— **Elva Ainsworth**, Founder and CEO, Talent Innovations

'A refreshingly accessible read, full of insights and exercises that both re-frames the concept of ego, and re-tools us accordingly.'

— **Penny De Valk**, Leadership Coach and Mentor

'If you want to lead high-performing teams, you need to notice yourself and the impact that you have on others. On that journey, this book is a must read. Mary blends theory, real-world examples and practical points of reflection to raise awareness of ego: yours and that of the people that you lead.

It will help you to understand your ego and how you react. To be more aware of others' egos, and how to adapt your approach to their needs. Working with Mary helped me to understand myself better, and to build authentic relationships with colleagues. Mary has captured the essence of that coaching in this excellent book.'

— **Ed Garcez**, Chief Digital and Information Officer (London Borough of Camden)

RETHINK PRESS

First published in Great Britain in 2020
by Rethink Press (www.rethinkpress.com)

ego

GET OVER YOURSELF AND LEAD

Mary Gregory

Introduction

Much is expected of leaders today, in particular enabling high performance and engaging others. That phrase on paper may seem straightforward, but building relationships, encouraging people to come with us and enabling them to fulfil their potential is far from that. There are multiple dimensions at play, riddled with opportunities that can challenge and stretch us, make us question ourselves, feel frustrated or joyful. It would be so easy if everyone was just like us, but it's the diversity of different personalities and backgrounds that makes for a rich world and successful organisations.

This book is all about building relationships and how we manage ourselves, learning to recognise and get over our ego as we strive to navigate the organisations in which we work. Its basis comes from many lessons I've learned in supporting leaders in all types of organisations to get the best out of others and maximise their influence. In the book, I include many real-life examples, from addressing poor performance to giving feedback to a senior leader, to shifting one's personal perspective. I also share insights from my own journey. We all have our ego and the potential to let it get in our own way. Being a coach and consultant doesn't make me immune to that.

Ego gets a lot of bad press. Yes, there are elements to our ego that are unhelpful and even destructive to both ourselves and others, but it is not always easy to separate ourselves from our ego, and as it's designed to protect us there are times when it is unhelpful to do so. When leading, we do need to get over ourselves and transcend the elements of our ego that get in the way of taking courageous action or building authentic relationships and creating psychologically safe working environments.

I have designed the book to firstly show you how ego can stand in your way so you can spot the signs. This means there is the opportunity to do some self-exploration, as well as consider frameworks my clients and I have found invaluable in understanding what is going on in both our relationships and the wider organisations of which we are a part. We will then explore what you can do about it.

Leadership in organisations today is not for the faint hearted. It takes courage to lead, and it takes courage to look into yourself openly and honestly so that you can lead with greater authenticity. By looking to yourself and the energy you create around you, you can not only discover how to address immediate challenges, but also build your level of consciousness to ensure you lead from a place of increased power and personal confidence. By strengthening your own sense of your authentic self and understanding the dynamics at play in human relationships, you will be able to lead by connecting and engaging with others effectively.

This book is about enabling change from the perspective of truly engaging and bringing others on board so they are motivated to perform at a high level and make that change happen. Underpinning that is the need for us as leaders to be aware of our own egos and how to manage ourselves, while being conscious of others' egos and how to influence and work with them. In summary, it addresses how we manage ourselves and others from an ego perspective to the benefit of all.

You will find each chapter structured to help you follow and reference it easily, with a 'We'll explore' section at the start, outlining the concept we'll look at over the course of the chapter, and a summary at the end, offering pertinent points of reflection. Throughout the chapters, I will bring the subject to life with reality checks, illustrating ideas and concepts with situations

I'm sure will be familiar to many of you, and exercises so you can get involved and put the ideas into action.

Let's get started by asking a fundamental question – what *is* ego?

1
What Is Ego?

We'll explore:

- What's behind our emotional reactions?
- What do I mean by ego?
- How ego does and doesn't serve us
- Learning to manage ego

What's behind our emotional reactions?

Consider these scenarios:

REALITY CHECK

In which four different reactions come from the ego

Scenario 1: I walk into the room where the leadership programme will be taking place. The room is prepared boardroom-style with tables and chairs, projector, screen. This is not what I asked for. This is to be a rolling programme with many different groups and there have been several conversations about how the room needs laying out, so I feel annoyed and irritated. How many times does it take for the message to get through? Is this organisation incompetent? The voice in my head sounds superior and critical and this adds to my sense of frustration, but my assumptions, based on my opinion, are correct.

Scenario 2: Jennifer offers feedback to a senior director. His tone aggressive, he challenges what she says. Jennifer hesitates, and then backtracks. What she has to offer is a valid observation, but as he can influence her job and career, she clearly feels frightened about upsetting him. She also feels powerless, helpless and annoyed at herself for misjudging how she communicated the message.

Scenario 3: Chris has told me he wants his team to participate more and come up with ideas in the meeting. His intention is to sit back, listen and encourage others to speak. Early in the meeting, I can see him becoming concerned that his people are not speaking up, and before long, he is interrupting, jumping in with his knowledge and suggestions, and the meeting returns to its usual pattern with Chris doing most of the idea generation. Afterwards, he reflects with me on what happened and how, despite his intentions to the contrary, the meeting took the familiar course of all his team meetings, where he dominates proceedings.

Scenario 4: Frances has told me that, yet again, she is concerned by a team member's performance. They are unwilling to take on anything extra, unhelpful to colleagues and the quality of their work is not up to scratch. Frances is conscious she must speak to them, but she hasn't. There are so many other things she needs to do, so she prioritises her list and decides to leave it another week before approaching them. Several weeks pass and Frances still has not found the time.

All the above are reactions coming from the ego. In each example, there were good reasons why each person responded as they did. From my own point of view, it was the desire to ensure the best environment for the participants in my programme. Jennifer's career was important to her and she wanted to keep on the right side of her boss. Chris really wanted his team to participate, but he was more concerned about generating ideas. Frances, on the other hand, was feeling the pressure from her competing priorities. Her lack of confidence in handling a tricky conversation meant her unconscious ego drove her to de-prioritise and avoid a stretching situation.

We can frequently rationalise why we do or don't do something. Often, we put that reason outside of ourselves, blaming others and our circumstances as being what's behind our reaction and emotional response. It's much easier to do that than to take a look at ourselves and how we might be contributing to a situation.

In the moment, our emotional reactions can make us feel important and give us a false sense of power. My blaming the organisation gave me a sense of self-righteousness, but making the other party wrong in this way doesn't result in real power or, indeed, the ability to

many years. On the one hand, this can be helpful – after all, we have survived. On the other hand, ways that worked for us in the past don't necessarily work for us in the present, particularly if we are playing a different and bigger game. How much do you want a decision you made at the age of three to be running the show now? Our well-developed ego-based survival strategies can end up holding us back, impacting others and what they think of us, and inhibiting our ability to act in a powerful, authentic way.

REALITY CHECK

In which Harry wants his team to participate more

Harry is concerned that all the idea generation is done by him in meetings and his team members don't contribute enough. I agree to observe one of his team meetings, during which Harry is friendly and warm, but dominates the conversation with intriguing stories from his experience. It is clear he already has ideas for how to address the issues he said he wanted his team's input on.

When a member of his team does contribute some original thinking, Harry quickly points out why it wouldn't work. This team member withdraws and doesn't make any further contributions, possibly feeling humiliated or demeaned. There is an uncomfortable atmosphere in the room. The rest of the team nod in agreement with all of Harry's ideas; there is no debate, as people shuffle in their seats, check the clock and appear to be dying for the meeting to end.

Afterwards, Harry says he feels frustrated by the over-compliance of his team.

This reality check illustrates some of the different ways our egos can be at play and get in the way. Harry is well intentioned; he wants his team to contribute, but he is an ideas person and his need to express his ideas, linked to his fear of not generating the solutions he is seeking, means he is impatient and jumps in, dominating the meeting and not allowing space for people to think, let alone contribute. When a team member does make a contribution, Harry is so fixed on his own ideas, he is unable to accept an alternative view. There's a good chance that the team member who contributed will have felt deflated and their own ego reaction is to withdraw. The rest of the team falls into compliance – another ego strategy for keeping ourselves safe.

This is a classic example of how our ego can get in the way of us achieving what we really want. It also shows how different ego reactions can bounce off each other.

EXERCISE

Think of an example where you found yourself reacting in a way that was domineering or withdrawing.

What can you understand about your own ego and how it impacts you?

How might it be impacting on those around you?

How ego does and doesn't serve us

It's valuable to accept that our ego is part of us, our identity and psyche. Unless we have an ambition to be a Yogi or Buddhist monk, it is always going to be with us in some form. Ego protects us from feelings of anxiety, influencing others to do things that work for us, enabling us to experience a sense of comfort and familiarity. For example, although Harry wanted his team to contribute, he was attached to his own ideas so his ego kicked in and dominated the meeting. His team duly reciprocated by withdrawing or complying with him.

The challenge with our ego is that we have learned survival strategies which worked once, but don't necessarily work for us now. When we are babies, it's acceptable for us to consider that the world revolves around us, but as we mature and become socialised, our ego-centredness ceases to serve us as it once did. But we still need to navigate through our careers, lives and relationships, all of which will present circumstances that challenge our sense of self and cause us to react according to the survival strategies we learned as children.

Most of the time, our ego keeps us safe and in our comfort zone. Made up of a large selection of habits which have become embedded to the point of being reactionary, our ego enables us to deal with the anxiety that is activated moment by moment as we navigate our daily lives.

These habits are supported by a set of beliefs, established in our childhood as a means of survival. They worked well for us then, and may work well for us in our adult lives, but we can also outgrow our habits. As we strive to be good leaders, the same habits that supported us in our early years can hold us back as we navigate the often complex and political terrain of organisational life.

REALITY CHECK

In which survival strategies are not working anymore

Scenario 1: I learned as a child that I would get praised and loved for making sure everyone else was OK. Feeling loved and acknowledged makes me feel good, so my ego strategy developed a set of beliefs and behaviours all about pleasing others. As an adult, I work hard, putting in more time than necessary supporting and helping others, but not so much looking after myself. I then find I get overlooked for a longed-for promotion. Because I am so busy taking care of everyone else, I neglect my own ambitions. I hide my light under a bushel. A strategy that helped me as a child does not help me now.

Scenario 2: I enjoy the acknowledgement I get for doing good work and being a straight-A student. Deciding (unconsciously) that this is something I will always strive for – my excellent abilities will never be brought into question – I progress quickly in my career and appreciate being considered a high flier. I become the youngest director in my company, but suddenly I find I am struggling to get others to achieve to my high standards.

> Scenario 3: In my family, we always prided ourselves
> on being resilient and as I grew up we dealt with many
> challenges without complaint. As a leader, I am com-
> pletely self-reliant. Rather than seek support or admit
> I am challenged, I push my team hard and do whatever
> I can to cover any shortfall so that they, and I, look
> good. But my strategy of always delivering excellence
> is fragmenting as the demands of a recent promotion
> take their toll. I start to feel stressed.

As this reality check shows, ego keeps us safe, enables
us to survive, but it can also trap us into unhelpful
ways of being which have an impact on our behaviours
and the people around us.

Common ego traps

We fall into ego traps because we get something out of
them, but they also hold us back and can cause more
anxiety than we are trying to allay. Overtly, our ego
traps can demonstrate an over inflation or under inflation of our personal power and sense of importance.
They are habitual ways of being, although we may be
consciously or unconsciously using them as a means to
cover up a more vulnerable sense of self underneath.

Over-inflated	Under-inflated
Do it now!	People pleasing
Solo flight	Never good enough
I'm alright, Jack	Rescue me!
Blaming others	Being cautious

Do it now! When this part of our ego kicks in, we need to sort everything out as quickly as possible. It's linked to our impulsive drives and need for immediate gratification, is forceful and means we avoid having to think.

If we're taking action, we get a sense of reassurance from doing something, even though we might not have planned or prioritised it. This part of our self risks unfocused or even reckless action, wasting our personal resources, and it can lead to exhaustion. When caught in this ego trap, we inhibit our own and others' thinking, limiting opportunity for learning and innovation. People around us may feel coerced and therefore won't fully engage.

Solo flight. Those of us who are familiar with the ego trap of solo flight will place importance on self-reliance and will appear to others as consistently resilient and capable. Asking for help is unacceptable as we constantly strive to be the one who can sort it all out. If we're caught in this trap, admitting vulnerability and that we need help will be excruciating.

Putting on a show of constant strength can lead to burnout. Being invulnerable also impairs our ability to build mutually supportive relationships and create the psychological safety which is so important when creating open, honest, high-trusting organisational cultures where people can perform at their best.

15

I'm alright, Jack. Smugness dominates this ego trap. When we are caught up in it, we resist feedback, believing we are correct (and others are incorrect). We don't see any good reason to change and are generally content with ourselves; it's everyone else who has 'issues'. The risk is that we don't empathise with others, staying aloof, even superior, and indirectly communicating we don't really care. This then creates disconnection and mistrust in relationships.

Unfortunately, organisations can encourage this ego trap in their leaders. As a leader becomes more senior, the privileges given to them increase, for example the executive suite, their own PAs, which potentially can feed a sense of power and superiority. Lack of openness to feedback results in people being less likely to be fully open, creating a culture where leaders potentially act in increased isolation and with a lack of appreciation of what is really going on in their organisations.

Blaming others. When it's too anxiety-provoking to accept our responsibility in something, we will point the finger and blame others. This can take place on an individual basis, eg blaming our partner for our unhappiness, or on a generalised – even global – scale, blaming a whole group for causing our problems, eg blaming our team for missing a target.

In this trap, we don't take responsibility. The person or people we're blaming may be at fault, but other factors may also have contributed to the issue, eg lack of resources or poor delegation. What we risk with blaming others is not getting to the root cause of the problem so mistakes are repeated, creating a climate of fear where people feel anxious and avoid taking responsibility

People pleasing. Many of us have been brought up to be polite and make sure everyone around us is kept happy. We get a sense of self-esteem by ensuring harmony, believing we've done something that has really supported and helped someone else. On the downside, we may find it excruciating or even paralysing to ask for our own needs to be met or to stand up to someone if we fear it will upset them.

This ego trap risks communication being withheld and a lack of honesty, leading to misunderstandings and upsets.

Never good enough. No matter how well someone or a team or group has achieved something, we never feel satisfied and constantly strive to make it better, possibly to the point where we risk wasting our resources of energy, time, people and money. The more we seek perfection, the more it eludes us. Standards are important, but not at the cost of exhausting and demoralising ourselves or those we lead.

Rescue me! When caught in this ego trap, we may feel overwhelmed and helpless, wanting others to sort things out for us, rather than being responsible for ourselves and deciding how we need to proceed. This means we over-rely on others and seek external solutions rather than accessing our internal resources.

The risk is that we potentially drain those around us. They may initially feel good about supporting us, but eventually they can feel used. For a leader, this way of being can be disconcerting to our teams and hinder a sense of clear purpose or direction.

Being cautious. When operating from the trap of being cautious, we hold a view that the world is unsafe, resulting in a lack of trust in others and the world generally. This serves to protect us and keep us safe, but being overly cautious leads to stagnation and inertia. We take too long to make decisions or make them at too high a level. This can undermine the motivation, confidence and potential of those we lead.

As all these traps show, while we need our ego, allowing our over or under inflated ego to dominate is not going to help us as a leader. We need to find ways to transcend our ego traps. Not doing so can result in us alienating others and sabotaging ourselves and the results we want to achieve. Knowing how we can trap ourselves gives us access to different choices as to how we respond.

EXERCISE

Which of the ego traps resonates most strongly with you? How might you be acting based on strategies you developed in your past? How well are these serving you now? What would you like to change or modify?

It's not all about us. As well as learning to manage ourselves, we also need to manage others, something we have even less control over. To be effective at work, we require an awareness and sensitivity towards ourselves and those we are interacting with – a constant scanning between our own internal state and the reactions and responses of others externally.

This is no mean task, but it is possible. The leaders I've come across who are the most effective tend to have the ability to notice themselves *and* the people they are impacting, and modify their approach to meet with the demands of the people and ego/s they may be dealing with.

From what I observe from myself and working with leaders, navigating our own ego and those of others is at the hub of being an effective leader and creating workplaces that bring out the best in everyone. To make sustainable change happen, we need to get to the source of how we empower or limit ourselves, and ego is right there in the centre.

Learning to manage ego takes time

Learning to understand and manage our ego takes commitment; it is not a straightforward journey and is often one that we can veer away from in search of 'quick fixes' that don't last.

We would not go to the gym, participate in a two-hour workout, and then expect our level of fitness and body to transform. Similarly, developing ourselves, opening up our self- and social-awareness, refining our way of being, comes from an intentional practice which is ongoing over time. Just as we see progress with our physical fitness when we embark on an exercise regime, so we will gain personal power and confidence along the way.

From experiencing my own journey and supporting others with theirs, I've learned the source of real, sustainable change lies in getting to the things within us that hold us back and using our strengths and insights to turn them around. We then learn how to manage our anxieties and fears, and consciously enhance the impact we have on others.

We need to focus on what we do well to recognise our strengths. This is not about massaging our ego, but responsibly owning the things we are good at so we can contribute fully to our own and others' success. Our ego can sometimes be our own worst enemy, not allowing us to accept the things we are good at, adeptly putting us down instead. Hands up if you have an inner critic, alive and well and living inside your head? Navigating our ego requires us to shift our limiting beliefs and reactions while acknowledging and working with our capabilities. The two are not mutually exclusive; in fact, they interact closely. For example, my strength of being able to engage an audience can become a weakness if I overplay the presentation and it becomes all about the performance I'm giving and loses touch with what the audience wants.

I've often heard the skills of managing ourselves and our impact on others described disparagingly within organisations as soft skills or 'pink fluffy bits', but it's actually those skills and levels of awareness that make the difference in leaders and organisations being effective. As one task-focused engineer I worked with said as he suddenly appreciated the impact of his behaviours on others: 'Actually, soft skills are really the hard skills.'

They're hard because they take a certain level of consciousness, focus and energy to develop, and because they are the skills that make the difference in how effectively we engage and enable performance in others. What I mean by 'engage' in this context is the emotional connection where people are more than merely buying into the purpose and direction of the company they work for; they actively feel part of it. They know their contribution matters and the company values have meaning for them to the point that they own and take responsibility for their performance. In other words, there is a jointly shared ownership within the company that is bigger than the individual egos.

The tricky thing with ego is that unless we have developed a level of self-awareness, it is something we are often unconscious of, resulting in us not having much control over it. As part of our personality, our ego has been shaped by our experiences and the behavioural habits we developed while growing up. Fed by core beliefs and values, these habits are often firmly embedded. Some are helpful and support us in our success, but others hold us back and create results we don't want. Our ego provides us with our sense of identity and personality, an array of skills, behaviours and attributes, but it also influences our wellbeing and confidence in ourselves, which includes reactive behaviours and attitudes that are not always helpful to either us or others. The good news is these habits can be changed. I will guide you throughout the pages of this book to learn how to manage your own ego, and those of others.

Summary

Our ego is part of being human. It is a learned survival strategy which becomes risky when over or under inflated. It is most obviously in evidence when we are dominating others, being self-righteous, or making others wrong and holding a sense of superiority about our view. But it is equally present when we withdraw, make ourselves small, feel self-conscious or allow our own internal critic to dominate.

The strategies we embed in our ego as children do not necessarily serve us as leaders in the modern workplace. Taking time to learn about ourselves, noticing our strengths, potential vulnerabilities and how our ego behaviour can impact us and others gives us access to different ways of being that transcend our ego.

REFLECTION

How do you know when your ego is in control? Review this list of questions to help you identify when and where your ego is being activated. See how many of these signs you can relate to yourself, and you may well have other signs you can add.

Do you ever find yourself:

- Blaming others for your circumstances and why things aren't working?

- Enjoying a good gossip?

- Sticking with your point of view at all costs?

- Feeling misunderstood and sorry for yourself?

- Expecting others to come to your rescue and sort everything out for you?

- Taking over and sorting out other people's problems?

- Dying for an alcoholic drink or eating something like chocolate or engaging in some other activity to soothe or calm you?

- Feeling embarrassed?

- Working to the point of exhaustion?

- Rushing to get everything sorted as soon as possible?

- Reluctant to ask for help?

- Keeping hold of information that you know could help others to maintain a sense of power?

- Avoiding giving feedback for fear of what might happen?

- Wanting to win at all costs?

- Comparing yourself unfavourably to others?

- Being superior, judging and criticising others?

- Constantly seeking perfection?

- Feeling inadequate, like one day you will be found out?

- Feeling envious or jealous of other people's success?

- Getting upset when you lose, as opposed to looking for the learning?

Whichever questions you said yes to indicate how your own ego can show up when activated. There is no right or wrong in this, it just is what it is. What's helpful is to be conscious of the way your ego reacts is impacting you and the people you lead.

2
The Leader's Dilemma

We'll explore:

- Focus on task over behaviour
- The organisational terrain today
- Leadership is primarily about relationships
- The need for greater flexibility

REALITY CHECK

In which focusing on task dominates over addressing behaviour

Roy and his executive team had really enjoyed and gained from the two days they had taken out to work on themselves. Each of them was left feeling inspired, motivated and keen to take action, following up on agreed commitments and practising new behaviours.

Two weeks later, Roy was feeling disillusioned. Two members of his team had returned to the conflict he'd believed had been dealt with during the team

> workshop. Although there had been some change in the team members' attitude during their recent strategy meeting, they still seemed to be going round in circles in terms of pursuing the action to ensure the acute turnaround needed in the business.
>
> Despite best efforts to change, Roy and his team seemed to be rapidly returning to the status quo with high levels of focus on targets and ensuring these were met.

The demands of organisational life, with the ever-increasing agenda of change, quality service and improvements, rising profits or cost savings, mean that you may as a leader experience feeling under constant pressure, like Roy and his team. These circumstances increase the likelihood of reactive and often unhelpful ego-centred behaviour.

According to the Gallup survey 2017,[2] just under 70% of employees are either not engaged or actively disengaged. Gallup's definitions are:

- **Not engaged** – an employee is in 'checked-out' mode. They show up for work each day and do their tasks, but aren't passionate, innovative or making deeper contributions.

- **Actively disengaged** – these are employees who are deeply unhappy and/or acting out, possibly

---

2   Gallup (2017), State of the American Workplace, www.gallup.com/workplace/238085/state-american-workplace-report-2017.aspx

working against the organisation's objectives on daily basis.

Gallup describes certain elements that contribute to enabling engagement and are clearly linked to leadership behaviour. These include the need for people to be clear on what is expected of them, to understand how they contribute to the business's overall goals and, probably most importantly when it comes to leadership impact, to have strong relationships, feeling part of a team and experiencing their manager as genuinely caring about them.

I interpret this as a leader's ability to build relationships, which enhance confidence in those they lead, and a culture of safety and trust makes all the difference to levels of performance and organisational success. How we show up, the way we relate to ourselves and to others, our management of ourselves, our ego and our response to others all create our unique leadership style and ability to communicate directions and engage others to come with us.

It is well documented that people join an organisation they admire, but leave because of the way they have been managed and led.[3] This attrition costs the organisation not only in terms of time and money spent on recruiting, inducting and ultimately losing talent, but also on a strategic level as it is potentially damaging to

---

3   Buckingham, M and Coffman, C (2005) *First, Break All The Rules: What the world's greatest managers do differently.* London: Simon & Schuster

reputation, brand and creating an organisation fit for the future. The majority of leaders I come into contact with today are well-intentioned people, wanting to do a good job and make a positive difference. Their challenge is how to manage themselves, their beliefs and confidence to influence stakeholders and the performance of their teams, while navigating often complex and politically charged cultures and dynamics.

And this is the dilemma, the chicken and egg of the situation. Organisations are nothing more than a collection of human beings coming together with a common purpose and endeavour. Although they are populated by ordinary people, something happens when a group comes together as an organisation. The 2003 Canadian film *The Corporation* reviews the behaviour of large organisations from the perspective of psychological pathology and finds them to have the personality traits of a psychopath.[4]

This psychological condition is classified by:

* Superficial charm – psychopaths are initially engaging to others

* Lack of empathy and recognition or respect for the rights of others

* Focus on self – psychopaths put themselves and their own ego wants and needs first

---

4 *The Corporation* (2003), directed by Mark Achbar and Jennifer Abbot, written by Joel Bakan, Harold Crooks and Mark Achbar

- A disregard for rules and law

- Manipulative behaviours in pursuit of control and power

- Lack of remorse or guilt for action

- A tendency to display abusive or violent behaviours, particularly if their fragile ego is slighted or threatened in any way

We have all probably got stories of leaders who have narcissistic or psychopathic tendencies, and there are many more who cause a scandal and hit the headlines in the press, but from my experience of working in organisations over the last couple of decades, while people with these character traits do exist, I have come across far more organisations led by people who don't fall into this category. So what happens within the organisation to result in a collective set of behaviours that is so far removed from humanity?

Focus on task over behaviour

Ultimately, whether it's in the private or public sector, an organisation has a result it is trying to achieve for a variety of stakeholders. This may be providing the best value to taxpayers, quality of service or product to customers, or profits for shareholders. This means that the task, or what the organisation is there to do, dominates attention. In comparison, behaviour, or how people are being, is given attention almost reluctantly. Meetings are consumed by discussions about task; processes are constantly streamlined in service of task; the majority of activity is all about what the organisation needs to do to get the job done.

As leaders, managers or team members, we can easily find ourselves on the hamster's wheel of 'do, do and do some more', relentlessly busy with activity to ensure the task gets done. There is little or no time for activities that support enhancing performance, such as coaching conversations, reflection or considering strategy. Things are out of kilter.

The over focus on task and pressure to deliver tends to result in a cultural disconnect between head and heart, with a cold focus on the short-term results of the bottom line rather than the far-reaching, longer-term impact and contribution the organisation could create. Don't get me wrong, I'm not saying an organisation shouldn't be making a profit or spending the public purse responsibly. What I am suggesting is the over focus on task results in a business culture that is non-holistic and neglects the many positive human qualities that create great places to work and enhance performance. This lack of attention to human behaviour and the cultural climate makes the workplace ripe for our egos to play out and utilise our well-worn survival strategies.

Part of the leader's role is to create the circumstances that ensure optimum engagement and performance, yet what often happens is that leaders create circumstances that challenge people's ability to perform, and can even be damaging to it. For example, the most common complaint I hear from leaders and their teams across all sectors and types of organisation is 'We are dealing with an ever-increasing workload, fast-moving change and shifting priorities, and constantly needing to do more with less'. The effect is that people experience stress and exhaustion, and in such a state we are much more vulnerable to our ego traps. Leaders may become increasingly isolated from what is going on 'on the ground' in their organisations, and people don't push back because they are caught up in a survival mode. Culture and ego survival strategies keep these challenging circumstances in place and can create a 'learned helplessness' around them.

Even in organisations that already have a relatively sophisticated perspective on performance, task still usurps consideration of how people are being and working together. I have observed more than one organisation put in place a specially designed process to support and encourage leaders to step back and look at how they and their teams have performed, only for that process to become a task in itself. Treated like a tick-box exercise, it is completed as quickly as possible with little if any exploration or learning.

Breaking habits isn't easy. Focusing on the task, which is external to ourselves, feels so much more comfortable than self-reflection, yet our ego's avoidance of discomfort leads to many missed opportunities. The fallout is the loss of valuable insights, learning and innovations that could enhance performance.

Other processes also often contradict what the organisation is espousing to be important. For example, being 'people focused' is a popular organisational value, yet all targets tend to relate to sales or cost saving and have nothing to do with how a leader has led their team. If this is what a leader is measured on, then it is where they are going to put their attention, creating a system and culture that is task focused and potentially psychopathic at the expense of embracing behaviours and attitudes that create real engagement and enhancement of performance.

The organisational terrain today

The landscape of organisations is changing. The advent of technology, the nature of each generation as they enter the workplace and world events all impact on the way in which we do business and behave.

Following the global financial crisis and subsequent recession of 2008, the term 'new normal' emerged as a way of describing the terrain in which organisations of all shapes and sizes existed. Once trusted institutions and practices were shown to be unreliable, taking away our sense of security and what we considered certain. Thus, a new age emerged, highlighted by the characteristics of VUCA:

- **V** – volatile

- **U** – uncertain

- **C** – complex

- **A** – ambiguous

The notion of VUCA was introduced by the US Army War College to describe the more volatile, uncertain, complex and ambiguous multilateral world that resulted from the end of the Cold War, but since 2008, it has also commonly referred to the constant change being faced by organisations.

Change was always at the forefront of most organisations' agenda, but now more than ever, leaders need to deal with the unexpected and navigate the implementation of tricky and complicated plans, which challenges their ego needs for safety and certainty. Dealing with high levels of uncertainty and complexity brought about by the new normal and VUCA is not a one-person job. It takes a supportive system with a high level of engagement and commitment from all on board, and a different kind of leadership behaviour creates this. No longer is the chief executive the one hero or heroine; from CEOs to front-line managers, leaders need to develop their ability to reach beyond themselves and engage with people, creating collaborative relationships and cohesively aligned teams that pull together and jointly rise to the challenges the new normal presents.

In his book *Leaders Make The Future: Ten new leadership skills for an uncertain world,*[5] Bob Johansen describes an antidote to VUCA which he calls 'positive VUCA':

V – vision. If you as a leader have vision, you have a frame of reference from which to navigate challenges and take each as an opportunity to move forward.

U – understanding. Create understanding through listening and finding out, learning from what is certain and uncertain. Use what you understand to create a sense of stability.

C – collaborative. Work with others, using the strengths of teams both internally and cross organisationally.

A – agile. Shift perspectives from the big picture to smaller details and back again. Entertain the possibility of whatever circumstances may present themselves.

I would go further. From my experience of working with outstanding leaders, I would say you also need to be:

---

5   Johansen, R (2012) *Leaders Make The Future: Ten new leadership skills for an uncertain world.* San Francisco: Berrett-Koehler. Model used here with kind permission of Bob Johansen.

V – vulnerable. Be willing to open up and be honest about your own journey and experiences. Be value centred, leading from your core values. This enables you to make decisions using your values as inner guideposts.

U – unrelenting in your commitment. Don't give up, but ensure you have the resilience to deal with ongoing challenges.

C – courageous. Be able to manage your fear and take action, however frightening this may seem at the time. Be candid, open, honest and transparent to support the development of trust and congruency.

A – assertive. Be willing to stand up for what you believe in, appreciative of others and their contributions and differences, and able to deal with uncertainty in a calm and balanced way. Be adult – we'll talk more about this later.

Johansen also talks about leaders letting go of their ego-centred need to be all powerful and in control while remaining transparent, open and willing to fully engage with others. The new normal requires the use of many minds and hearts to navigate it effectively, not just the one.

If the new normal is the terrain within which leaders now lead, then there are challenging and complex issues to address. These can't be solved quickly and easily; they are the 'wicked issues' that have been present for a long time and involve multiple agencies. For example, in the public sector, child safeguarding incorporates schools, police, social services, local government. In the corporate world, an organisation may be blind to the systems and processes that hold diversity and inclusion in place, and will need to make multiple interventions to address it.

One of the key qualities of leaders when they're addressing such complex challenges is the ability to let go of always having to have the right answer. Instead, they need to get around the table with other parties to collaborate on creating a strategy that will tame the issue.

REALITY CHECK

In which one organisation in the system recognises how their collective ego is impacting finding a solution

During the Protestant Orange marches through a Catholic community in a town in Northern Ireland, year on year, tensions spilled over into fights and trouble. The police were constantly trying to find a solution to bring peace between the two communities, but it wasn't until they recognised that their attitude and approach were part of the issue impacting the overall dynamic that they made real progress. On seeing this, they were then able to take responsibility for how their behaviour was contributing to the situation and join with all parties around the table to create a jointly owned and shared solution.

> The police moved from seeing the problem as outside
> of themselves to recognising that they were part of
> it. Starting with the senior leaders in the force, they
> collectively managed their organisational ego. Only
> when they made this distinction did they shift their
> behaviour and attitude. In other words, they got out of
> their own way, which had a profound impact on them
> being able to make a difference.

It took a leap of faith for the police to move in this way. They demonstrated candidness and vulnerability to take the action they did. To address tricky, complex change, leaders need to be in touch with their feelings, both positive and negative, be courageous enough to confront fears in the face of adversity, and be able to work with others collaboratively. Being able to join with others – side by side instead of separating, pointing the finger, blaming or fixing others – is one way that our ego can be transcended.

Leadership is primarily about relationships

I've worked with many leaders, from CEOs to rising stars, working for public sector organisations and a broad range of companies in the private sector, who wanted their managers to create high performance, embed cultural change and turn around company performance. All had their own specific needs and outcomes, but one common denominator emerged that separated the great leaders from the good, and that was the ability to manage and lead themselves first before they started to build sustainable authentic relationships.

Leadership is ultimately a relational activity. Relational leadership is where the leader focuses on creating positive relationships with the people they influence and impact, be it their team, stakeholders or line. Being a relational leader means going beyond yourself and your own ego-driven self-interest and being genuinely interested in understanding the motivation and needs of others. If you practise relational leadership, you achieve goals through building inclusive, empowering, purposeful relationships, underpinned by a foundation of integrity. This means being aware of yourself, your own ego traps and reactions, and the impact these have. It means being responsible for your actions and behaviour, being conscious of others and how to adapt your approach in tune with their needs.

Having an inspiring personality is not enough. The ability to connect authentically with others, to appreciate and empathise with their experiences, is the often-missing ingredient to really being able to take people with you. And to be able to get that level of relationship means letting go of your own ego-centred focus. Leaders who achieve this unlock the potential to build relationships that engage and empower others.

REALITY CHECK

In which Alison has to get over herself to address performance

I recall coaching Alison, a recently promoted senior executive, who needed to address Giles, one of her team members who was underperforming. Alison was anxious about approaching Giles, particularly as he had been one of her peers until recently.

By building her understanding of her relationship with Giles and how this had now changed, and giving consideration to her own behaviour and how she needed to be when she had the conversation with him, Alison was able to be honest and authentic with Giles, acknowledging the change in their relationship and her responsibilities as leader. This opened up supportive dialogue that resulted in Alison successfully addressing the issue while further developing the relationship with Giles. He ultimately became a committed high performer whom she could trust implicitly.

Alison's line and HR partner were impressed with the turnaround she had achieved with Giles's performance. Her predecessor had avoided the courageous conversation, anticipating that Giles would leave or have to be put on performance measures. As a result, Alison's reputation as a leader who could bring out the best in people began to grow.

When leaders focus on the relationship as well as the task, their impact is more far reaching than just achieving the immediate result. If she'd been purely task focused, Alison's attitude in the conversation might have been much more confrontational and insensitive to Giles's feelings. While this may have led to a short-term improvement in his performance around the task, it would not have increased his sense of engagement, commitment and enjoyment. Alison's awareness of herself and ability to get over whatever anxiety she had about the conversation, along with her sensitivity towards Giles, meant she conducted the conversation in a respectful way that balanced logic and compassion. She managed her own ego, and her respect for Giles influenced his engagement in the conversation.

The need for greater flexibility

The need for a flexible and relational style of leadership is increasing as the workforce becomes more diverse. More than ever before, there is a widening of the generations working together across organisations. Millennials have entered the workplace with Generation Z hot on their heels, both bringing fresh energy and different perspectives. Generation X are well placed and often leading at senior levels, while Baby Boomers are still present thanks to the increasing retirement age, and may well be around for some time to come.

The table below highlights the common preferences and needs of each generational personality. This demonstrates how much leaders need to learn to flex and adapt their approach to tune in to the diversity of talent they now lead.

	Baby Boomers	Generation X	Millennials	Generation Z
	Born 1946–1964	Born 1965–1980	Born 1981–1995	Born 1996–2010
What makes me feel good?	I want my security needs met first – money, status, etc.	I look for autonomy – freedom is the ultimate reward.	I need work that is meaningful to me now.	I want a safe working environment, connection with people and a twist of technology.
Living my life	Help me balance other elements and find meaning outside of work.	I want work-life balance now, not at sixty-five.	I enjoy many activities, which means flexibility is key.	Work/life balance is a priority, please respect my hours.
Career attitude	I prefer a career trajectory, staying a reasonable time in one organisation.	Opportunity is king so I change jobs as I need to.	For me, there's no such thing as a job for life. Changing is part of my regular routine.	Financial independence is a career goal, but so is making a difference to the world.
How am I doing?	An annual appraisal is what I'm used to.	I would really like to know how I'm doing. Can you tell me now, please?	I need constant and immediate feedback. Using technology for this is fine.	Daily check-ins whenever possible, with clear, tangible measures.
Learning and growing	I like training in moderation.	The more opportunity I have to learn, the better.	Continuous learning is my way of life.	I embrace failure as a great opportunity to learn.

Each generation has its own footprint. More than ever, leaders need to be flexible and appreciate the differing requirements of the generations.

Generation Z are the first generation to have grown up with all social media platforms, but at the same time they have a huge need for real people connection. They can cope with honest feedback and see failure as an opportunity to learn. Millennials are also highly relational and collaborative, seeking constant feedback. These differences can place demands on a leader from a different generation. For example, a Baby Boomer leader will be used to more minimal feedback, so I'm sure you can imagine the challenges this could create if a Baby Boomer is the leader of a Millennial, or vice versa. Leaders need to tune in to the needs of each generation and adapt their approach accordingly.

Summary

Historically, organisations and the people who lead them focus on the task and what there is to do, rather than how they are being and the quality of behaviour and impact. The organisational terrain has changed, and is continuing to do so at a rate that is not going to slow down. Add further complexity and ambiguity to this and you require a modified style of leadership, one based on collaboration and agility. A leader needs to transcend ego to build really strong and effective relationships.

The personalities of the workforce are becoming more diverse, adding to the need for leaders to tune in to others effectively and flex their style accordingly.

REFLECTION

Think about the organisation you work in now, or ones where you've worked in the past:

- How much does getting the job done vs how you act and behave dominate the conversation and action?

- How volatile, uncertain, complex and ambiguous is the work terrain in the organisation? And how is this impacting you?

- Think of six colleagues and identify the style of leadership they need.

- What could you do to expand your range of behaviours?

3
Leading Others Means Leading Yourself First

We'll explore:

- Leadership influence
- Looking inside yourself

Never underestimate the influence and impact you are having as a leader in your field of work or life.

For a while, I lived an equal distance from two local supermarkets owned by the same supermarket chain. The two shops were a similar size and held the same products, representing the same brand values, so I would have expected to receive the same quality and delivery of service. But my experience in each store was quite different.

In Store A, I found the staff friendly and helpful, going out of their way to check the stock if what I wanted wasn't on the shelves. The checkout assistants always had a friendly chat with me at the till and helped me to the car if I needed it. I consistently left that store feeling happier than when I went in, and it was all due to the way the staff connected with me as a customer.

Store B, on the other hand, was almost the complete opposite. Yes, I could get what I needed purchase-wise, but when I asked for help the response was brusque. It was as if I was being a nuisance by asking, and I was lucky to get so much as eye contact from the person at the till. The whole atmosphere was different, and when visiting that store, I made sure I got in and out of it as quickly as possible.

Let's consider the difference. The staff in Store A demonstrated a real care and commitment to looking after their customers, and as a result it was a pleasure to shop there, which made me want to return. This was the impact they had, while at Store B, the staff acted like they couldn't be bothered. The impact of their uninterested behaviour was that the whole experience of shopping there was unpleasant and if I could have gone somewhere else, I would have done.

From both these examples, we can see the impact behaviour has, in this instance on the customer. Now consider the impact you have on the people you lead. From the examples of Stores A and B, I would suggest that the managers had different leadership styles and related to their teams in different ways.

REALITY CHECK

In which two leaders have contrasting styles and impacts

David was really interested in his people, supporting and coaching his department heads who'd then pass this approach on to how they led and managed their teams. People liked to work under David; they felt supported and trusted, and the impact of this was they would go out of their way in their work.

John, on the other hand, took a much more 'just do it' attitude. He liked people on his team to be like him and wasn't bothered about getting to know and understand them. John did what needed to be done, seeing it more as a chore than a means to develop and support his people. He went out of his way to look good and cover up mistakes made by himself or his team.

Both David and John possessed impressive records of achieving their targets year on year, but John had a higher than average turnover on his team. His reputation meant that people around the business dreaded, and in some cases actively avoided, being moved into his area. Those who did work for him successfully adopted his style of leading – even, quite curiously, to the extent of wearing similar clothes and taking on a strikingly similar physical presence.

This reality check demonstrates that how you show up as a leader has an impact on those around you. David was genuinely there for his team. He connected with them on a human level and built authentically supportive relationships. John, on the other hand, cast a shadow over the climate and atmosphere in his department. He focused wholly on getting the results that would make him look good, building superficial relationships and moulding people in his own ilk. Each leader impacted their people's levels of commitment, engagement and ability to perform at their best.

Leadership influence

Research conducted by Daniel Goleman in conjunction with Hay McBer, the consultancy he was working with, found that the climate within which people work accounts for a third of an organisation's results. In the same research, Goleman also identified that leadership behaviour has a positive or negative effect on climate.[6] The influence you have as a leader is much greater than you may imagine. It is happening all the time, sometimes at a microscopic level, but it is the difference that creates great places to work and sustains high performance. Both David and John delivered on company targets, but while John achieved targets year on year, the costs of staff turnover in terms of recruitment and induction would have been much higher than David's, as would the hidden costs of people's performance being impacted by fear and lack of engagement.

---

6   Goleman, D (2000) 'Leadership That Gets Results'. *Harvard Business Review*, March – April, https://hbr.org/2000/03/leadership-that-gets-results

As a leader in any context, when we're being effective, really engaging and building authentic relationships, we transcend our ego and shine a light on our team. This is supportive, inspiring and empowering. On the other hand, when we're reacting unconsciously from our ego's emotions, prejudices and biases, our behaviour casts a shadow which impacts others. This can result in fear, lack of trust, resistance or over compliance.

An important part of our role as a leader is to leave people in a more resourced place than before they came into contact with us. Being more aware of our own motivation, behaviour and interactions, managing our mood and reactions, takes conscious effort, but it is a fundamental part of being a leader. The ego-centred 'my way or the highway' approach doesn't cut it in the VUCA workplace we now operate in.

More than ever, being an effective leader who has the conversations to enable high performance requires being able to build strong relationships that have a positive impact. To do this, you must manage yourself, your moods and reactions. People will either shrink in your wake, push against your ideas or be inspired to perform beyond expectations. Which response would you prefer?

The impact of your ego as leader becomes even more important the more senior you become. Why? Simply because the more senior you are as a leader, the more visible you are and the more people know about you. You have the capacity to come into contact with and touch more people, both directly and indirectly.

REALITY CHECK

In which a leader's behaviour impacts his team performance and he is unwilling to consider his impact

George was a senior director leading a division of over 700 personnel. He had many positive leadership qualities: he was a deep thinker who shared profound alternative perspectives that stretched and challenged people's thinking and inspired them to be relentless in how they approached problems.

The organisation of which George's division was a part prided itself on having a culture of meritocracy, but from my first dealings with George and his team, I felt there was a sense of fear and trepidation around him as a leader. People referred to George as if his word was law; what he said was what happened. His team spent precious energy working out how to present things to him and finding the best time and way to approach him, as George was not easy to pin down. He actively avoided opportunities for more personal contact where relationships could be built, priding himself on having a stern 'no nonsense' approach. People knew when he wasn't happy, but he never fully explained what he needed from them.

George's dilemma, and the reason he engaged with me, was that he was unhappy with how his executive board was performing as a team. There was conflict, in-fighting and a resistance to pull together. This resulted in a loss of performance, low trust and an atmosphere of anxiety. People were constantly looking over their shoulders and covering up mistakes.

As part of an ongoing conversation about his team, I asked George how the way he was being as a leader might be impacting them. He pushed back, claiming he felt like he was being put on the spot and it was his team he wanted sorting out, not himself. Pointing the finger clearly at 'them' as a board team, George was excluding himself from the issue, making it hard to address the team's performance. It was almost as if he'd mentally and emotionally resigned and separated himself from his team.

The team members were stuck in some tricky dynamics and they knew it. Some endeavoured to address this, but without George being willing to open up and reflect on the impact he was having, the team's ego games continued. These games stopped any real dialogue; one member in particular seemed subversive and would not be held accountable. A couple of others were highly committed to sorting out how they behaved, but the rest showed little interest, choosing to look after themselves. George, in the meantime, withdrew further and further, seemingly oblivious to or just not willing to look at the impact his behaviour was having.

This demonstrates how a leader's behaviour infiltrates and influences beyond any level of consciousness, and how the behaviour of senior leaders has a huge impact on the climate and culture of an organisation. You may think you are only influencing the people you come into direct contact with, but how you leave those people, whether it's in a resourced or un-resourced state, will then influence the impact they have on others. This is why the success of change programmes is often so dependent on senior leaders and sponsors not only buying into, but also embracing and role modelling the desired behaviours.

> **REALITY CHECK**
>
> **In which an organisation's expectations are for the leader to look to themselves first when there is underperformance on their team**
>
> A successful and fast-growing organisation took a different approach to ensuring high performance. If a leader's team was not performing in a particular way, it was an organisational expectation for the first port of call to be the leader themselves, rather than point the finger at the team or individuals. Whatever the issue, it was the leader's responsibility, and they needed to ask themselves how they were influencing it. This resulted in a culture that, while still results focused, enabled reflection, personal responsibility and coaching from leaders to their teams.

Look inside yourself

You want to make change happen? You want your people to perform at their optimum? You want high engagement? Rather than looking externally for the answers, the first place for you as a leader to look is inside yourself.

Ask yourself, 'How am I being that is impacting on what is going on here?' and when answering, don't just look at what you are doing or not doing. It's also about considering how you are being; the subtleness in your behaviour, underpinned by your attitude, beliefs and values, makes all the difference. Is your ego running the show? Are you covering up to look good or avoid being caught out? How much are you acting from automatic pilot, running well-embedded patterns of behaviour such as trying to please others, seek perfection, stay strong, sort everything out as quickly as possible? How in control of that part of yourself are you?

As human beings, despite developments in technology and addictions to social media, we still have a need for real and meaningful connections with others, and when we get that from someone, it can make all the difference to our emotional engagement and levels of commitment. Never has the people-skills side of leadership been more pertinent.

Think of a time when someone really listened to you and understood where you were coming from. I expect that level of understanding touched you to the core. It's like they got exactly who you are and what you were experiencing.

There is something powerful about being heard and understood. It validates who we are, building our own insights and understanding. It helps us develop our thinking and access something we might have previously been blind to. The potential this creates for organisations seeking ever higher levels of performance, engagement and innovation is enormous.

Summary

Leading others means focusing on the relationships we have with them. It means being willing to look to ourselves first and consider the impact we are having on others, and then be responsible for that. How others show up around us is a reflection of our leadership style.

The place to start looking is internally. How might our beliefs, values and judgements be shaping our experience and the experience of others?

In the next chapters, we'll look at strategies you can adopt and models and methods that will support you in opening up your eyes to how you lead. This will help you to ensure you lead from a place of increased self-awareness, consciousness and authenticity.

REFLECTION

Think about how you act and behave and the impact this has on those around you, positive or negative.

- What do you do that really supports creating a great working atmosphere?

- What might you be doing that could detract from this?

Think about the relationships you build with others.

- How much do you take the time to really listen and understand where the people you lead are coming from?

What could you do, or how could you be, that would make you even better at engaging with the people who work with you?

4
Taking Ourselves On

We'll explore:

- How to stop running on automatic pilot
- How becoming more conscious is a choice
- Revelling in stepping out of our comfort zone
- Recognising our internal imposter
- Engaging with failure as an opportunity to learn

Stop running on automatic pilot

With so much pace and multiple commitments, the workplace today can be like running on the treadmill. We sometimes feel like we have little if any control to turn down the speed or adjust the incline. No wonder executive burnout is a real concern.

The thing about the treadmill is it puts us into an almost trancelike state of busyness, moving us straight from one activity to another without any time to think, reflect or consider our plan. The risk is we end up functioning most of the time on automatic pilot, just surviving yet another tricky meeting or crisis. But this automatic trancelike state hinders our ability to perform at our best, and enable others to do the same. We are not conscious of our actions and their impact and we don't learn from our mistakes. Instead, we move from one set of challenging circumstances to another without any let-up, threatening our health and wellbeing as well as the quality of the results we achieve.

Acting from this place of non-awareness presents increased risks not only to our own wellbeing, but also the wellbeing of those around us and the results we all ultimately achieve. Something may happen which carries a valuable lesson for us, but being in automatic mode, we don't notice it. Then when we face a similar crisis, we react and deal with it as we did before, using up even more energy. The ultimate risk here is a breakdown – a message so loud and clear that we have to wake up to deal with it. But how different it can be if we ensure we are awake in the first place to learn the lesson, apply it and move on.

As leaders, we can't wait until something goes wrong before stepping back. It is too late then. We need to switch off our automatic pilot and take a good look at what's happening on a regular basis. And in waking up, we then need to ensure we have some honest conversations, the first one being with ourselves.

Consider:

- How often do you give yourself a chance to reflect and look at things from different perspectives?

- If you do this, how honest are you with yourself?

- How willing are you to take a look and see how you are being and the impact you have on those around you?

As a leader, you have a need and responsibility to genuinely wake up to a different level of consciousness. This means learning about yourself, the impact you have, and understanding and appreciating what is going on around you from the different perspectives of your team members and the context of the organisation for which you work. Commit to a journey of self-discovery on a regular basis and be willing to understand yourself authentically. How does your way of being help or hinder positive and supportive relationships with others? Only when you allow yourself to sit back, get present and reflect do you start to see things from a different perspective, appreciate your contribution to any given situation and give yourself a chance to act differently.

Reflection and stepping back are fundamental to strategic thinking. I do a lot of work with leaders who are rising to new heights within their organisations and having a different level of expectation placed on them. They are required to be more strategic in their thinking, to consider the bigger picture and their department's contribution to the organisation's progression, rather than the operational detail. Stepping back and taking time to reflect on a regular basis is one of the easiest ways to develop strategic thinking. It takes discipline and commitment to do, but it reaps rewards via the insights and understanding it creates for the leaders who regularly practise it.

This is more than just a behavioural development. It's not going through the motions, intending to listen to others ideas when actually you're distracted and mentally ticking off all the tasks you need to get done by lunchtime. It takes a real capacity to understand yourself, get to know your own ego drives and needs, and address the things that get in the way of you being able to build real relationships.

REALITY CHECK

In which the leader is well intentioned, but appears blind to how her ego dominates

Susan was a high-powered CEO. She knew what she wanted and she was determined in her approach to achieving it. This provided clarity and drive, which gave those she led focus and energy.

Her approach was to engage and consult with her immediate and broader team – a great start, which delighted people. Team members were willing to contribute, but it became clear Susan already knew what she wanted and had her own answers. She might ask one of her line managers for their opinion, but then she tended to disregard their response, resorting to her own point of view.

This had a dampening effect on Susan's team members, who were left wondering why they had been asked in the first place. As a result, by the time Susan and her directors announced their vision and strategy, there was already a level of disengagement and cynicism from her team.

What Susan demonstrated was what I would call 'behavioural tokenism'. On the one hand, she clearly wanted to hear from those around her, but while saying their views would be taken into account, she had her own point of view which she was already attached to. No surprise that she stuck with her own viewpoint at the cost of utilising the rich data her team had offered.

On the surface, Susan made all the right noises, but underneath, her own beliefs and values drove her towards only going with her own opinion. She was running on automatic pilot, never stopping to consider how her own beliefs and drives were unconsciously impacting the quality of engagement and connection with those she led. Her conversations were merely a token gesture towards being a consultative, inclusive leader, but their impact on those around her was to leave them feeling manipulated, used and discounted.

Becoming more conscious is a choice

How do you stop being on automatic pilot? Quite simply, it's a choice and you can make it as easy or complicated as you like.

There are various activities you can engage in that will support you to develop an increased level of consciousness around yourself and your impact. These include scheduling regular time to reflect, journaling, meditation or mindfulness, engaging with a thinking partner or learning group, being coached, reading relevant books (see Bibliography) and attending development programmes. All these things will support you to get to know yourself and be more present.

Schedule short periods of time on a regular basis to allow yourself to step back from your busy workload to journal, reflect or meditate. As little as fifteen minutes a day can support you to become more conscious of yourself and what is going on around you, and the investment of that time reaps benefits through helping you step away from automatic reactive behaviour.

Switching off automatic pilot can help you see things from a different perspective and develop insights you wouldn't otherwise have. In the reality check, Susan was acting with all good intentions, which helped her look good and impress her team and colleagues initially. The challenge for Susan was her attachment to her own views, which meant she ultimately counteracted her good intentions. This impacted trust, motivation and buy-in from her team.

This was a blind spot for Susan. Blind spots are part of the challenge for anyone in the position of leader.

As a leader, we sometimes think we need to be seen to do certain things – in Susan's case, it was consult with the team, but she did it with a lack of authenticity. This undermined her good intention. Finding out how we impact others provides us with much-needed information, increasing our awareness and choices as to how we go about interacting with and relating to them. In Susan's case, underneath the token consultation, believing she already had the right answer resulted in disingenuous and closed-minded behaviour – the complete opposite to what she was likely to have intended. If Susan had asked for and listened to feedback from her team, they would have had the chance to reveal this blind spot. She would then have been able to learn and develop her effectiveness as a leader.

Often what is revealed in blind spots is something that lies in our unconscious domain of 'I don't know what I don't know'. In uncovering them, not only do we give ourselves the chance to develop, we also increase our self-awareness, introducing ourselves to new ways of being that might not have been possible before.

Revel in stepping out of your comfort zone

It takes courage to step out of your comfort zone and open your eyes, but in doing so, you learn so much about yourself and the prejudices that hold you back. One of my teachers encouraged me to move towards the discomfort, which included getting to know and working with the person I felt least inclined to work with, because these are the people we can often learn most from.

Our comfort zone is really a habit zone. Staying in it can keep us stuck in habits and ways of being, influenced by our limiting beliefs and biases, which in turn negatively impact those we lead. In stepping out of it, we give ourselves the opportunity to grow, develop and positively influence those around us, learning more about what we are capable of. The late David Bowie summed this up when he described one of the secrets to his success, which was to always step a bit further out of his depth than he was used to. When he reached the point where his toes were just touching the bottom, that was about the right place to do his best work.[7]

When you're considering being courageous, it's helpful to think about what the word really means. People who act with courage are not without fear, but they don't allow their fear to control them. They learn to manage themselves and their doubts and uncertainties and act, taking their fear with them.

---

7   Interview with David Bowie taken from the film *Inspirations* (1997) by Michael Apted, www.imdb.com/title/tt0125249

When fear is present, it is always our ego kicking in, which is an indication that we have a human need. But there are times we must transcend our needs and fears to strive for something bigger than ourselves. When we allow fear to stop us, it not only holds us back from trying things that could provide us with a rich source of learning, it also stops us from finding out about our strengths and what we are good at.

EXERCISE

Consider what it is you are really afraid of:

- Fear of failure (confirming what you knew all along, but were trying to cover up)?

- Fear of success? Now you've really got something to live up to, how on earth can you sustain this?

- Fear of being found out? You believe you're not really that good, so when is everyone else going to see that?

- Anything else?

How much is your fear based on a concern for the future and something that hasn't happened yet? How much is your fear based on an experience in your past that didn't go as well as you wanted and therefore is holding you back?

If you are focused on the past or the future, this is an indication you are not present in your current reality. The past allows memories and decisions from previous experiences to colour your thinking. The future allows concern over what could happen, but hasn't happened yet, to hold you back. Both of these are stories and fantasies that form your perceptions and distort your experiences and behaviour through the filters you then put on.

The truth is that not all decisions you made in the past are helpful to you in the present, and the future is yet to be. Being present means there is only now, this moment.

Experiment with being in the moment:

- Focus your attention on right now. Let go of any past- or future-based thoughts and see what opens up.

- What do you see? What do you hear? How do you feel right now?

- Take some deep breaths and keep focusing on being present.

In being present, what opens up for you?

Recognising our internal imposter

The first three fears I outlined in the exercise relate to something that's talked about more and more in the context of being a successful executive and leader: imposter phenomenon.

Imposter phenomenon as a concept was first developed by Pauline Clance and Suzanne Imes.[8] It refers to how we relate to ourselves in a way that is potentially

8   Clance, P and Imes, S (1978) 'The Imposter Phenomenon in High Achieving Women: Dynamics and therapeutic intervention'. *Psychotherapy: Theory, Research and Practice*, Volume 15:3, Georgia State University

self-sabotaging, holding ourselves back by telling ourselves we're a fake, that we can't really do our job well. The good news is the awareness of our imposter means we are already successful. After all, how can we be found out as a fake or failure if we are not achieving anything? It's also a sign that we are in touch with ourselves. From experiencing our own doubts and anxieties, we are more likely to relate with compassion to the concerns and experiences of others.

On the downside, imposter phenomenon means we don't allow ourselves to enjoy our successes as well as we might. We may well be giving ourselves a hard time and holding ourselves back.

Anyone who is successful is likely to have an internal imposter, but it can have a particular hold over those of us who are part of a minority group. Why? Because part of the antidote to our internal imposter is to have a strong support network and the backing of a good mentor. Those in minority groups – women in leadership, ethnic minorities, those with alternative sexual orientation, for example – often struggle with their internal imposter more, simply because there are fewer people to relate to and seek support from. Our imposter thrives when we experience isolation, feeling we are on our own in our endeavours.

This is a strong argument for minority groups to have their own networks and programmes of development. A women-only leadership programme is not about excluding men; rather, it allows women the space and time to share at a level that wouldn't be possible if their male counterparts were present. As the workplace becomes increasingly diverse, the need for new ways of supporting each other becomes ever more apparent.

What exactly is our imposter? Our imposter is actually another representation of an ego trap and how our ego can hold us back. Recognising that it is part of ourselves, acknowledging it and managing ourselves accordingly will help to keep our imposter at bay. Another way to quieten our imposter is to recognise our strengths, keep stretching ourselves and develop a more empathetic internal voice.

EXERCISE

Think about a time on your journey to becoming who you are today when you overcame adversity. Use these questions to help you reflect, and note down:

- What were the circumstances?

- How did you react to them?

- How did you know what to do?

- Did you involve anyone else? If so, who and how did you engage with them?

- What happened as a result of how you responded?

- What was your contribution to this?

Review what you've written down and experiment with reading your words through someone else's eyes. Consider what each of these people would say about the skills, strengths and qualities they see in you:

- Your best friend

- A trusted colleague

- A complete stranger

- A leader you admire

Note what is coming through and acknowledge the strengths and qualities you possess. Remind yourself of these on a regular basis, read them through before you have to tackle a challenge, and use them to help quieten that fearful voice that wants to keep you playing small.

Engage with failure as an opportunity to learn

Leading with our eyes open involves embracing and learning from our successes and our failures. Being comfortable with failure makes us so much more able to try things out, experiment, innovate and create. It also makes us more approachable and authentic as leaders.

REALITY CHECK

In which I attend a company event where admission of failure was unacceptable

At the company briefing, the senior leaders were presenting about progress against results. People in the room knew that there had been some tough times during the year and that one large account had been lost to a competitor.

The senior leadership team chose to ignore this and talked about all the things that had gone well during the year, even jokingly saying, 'Any failures? No, we never have those.' While their intention may have been to boost morale and keep the whole presentation upbeat, the impact was that people felt a lack of trust in what their leaders said and a sense that it wasn't OK to make mistakes. Both of these contributed to an atmosphere of increased anxiety, the complete opposite to what the leaders had intended.

Being able to own up and say, 'I did that and it didn't work, and this is how I would approach it differently next time...' role models personal responsibility and an openness to learning. It also demonstrates authenticity and sends a message that it's OK to be yourself and be responsible for your mistakes, both of which help create psychological safety, a foundation for enabling high performance.

Leading with your eyes open is often the road less travelled and there may be times when you find it too uncomfortable. This is when it's worth reminding yourself that nothing is permanent. The discomfort is a sign you are working through something powerful and important, and by staying open to it you will deepen your learning and ultimately reap the benefits.

If something continues to bother you or cause you to react, consider that you still have further learning to come from it. Or if it's really concerning you, seek appropriate support. Reaching out to a colleague, mentor or coach is invaluable in deepening our understanding. Learning is not always immediate; it happens over time. Insights emerge sometimes when you least expect them, so staying conscious to your thoughts and reflections requires a level of tenacity if you are to gain most from your learning.

Summary

Internal change takes intentional and committed effort over time. As a leader, you are on a journey to create and cause something, be it hitting financial targets, developing a new initiative, growing a community, building an enterprise or contributing to the world being a better place. You need others to come with you, because what you are creating is too big to do on your own. To have people coming with you means being adept at building relationships that inspire and engage, so an important part of your journey is to keep looking to yourself and how you are being. What is causing both your successes and your failures? Be willing to learn and understand yourself and the impact you have on those around you.

REFLECTION

Think about how you act and behave and the impact this has on those around you, positive or negative.

- What do you do that really supports creating a great working atmosphere?

- What might you be doing that could detract from this?

Think about the relationships you build with others.

- How much do you take the time to really listen and understand where the people you lead are coming from?

- What could you do, or how could you be, that would make you even better at engaging with the people who work with you?

Now think about what you do that encourages you to be present and increase your capacity to deal with the here and now.

- How much regular quality time do you give yourself to reflect?

- What activity could you engage with that would encourage you to quieten your mind?

5
Frameworks For Understanding Ourselves

We'll explore:

- Who's OK? Looking at the underlying processes that contribute to our behaviour
- The roles our ego can take
- How to navigate the different egos
- How our ego states can contaminate our thinking

I'm going to be sharing with you a couple of the most valuable models I have used over the years. Feedback from the leaders I've worked with has told me that these models helped them most profoundly in keeping their ego balanced.

I am sharing these models here to provide you with the opportunity to extract from them whatever you may find useful when you're navigating your own and other people's egos. My intention is to present the elements of the models that I believe are useful to leaders today and so provide a lens through which you can take a look at your own and others' behaviour to gain helpful insights and ideas for how you may approach a variety of situations.

The first model starts by inviting you to consider what attitude or mindset you hold about yourself and others. This is helpful, because our perceptions colour our experience and ultimately the way we act and behave.

Who's OK?

Thomas A Harris, in his classic book *I'm OK – You're OK*,[9] originated a model based on the work of psychiatrist Eric Berne. This model illustrates four life positions we can commonly find ourselves in. Harris bases his model on our overall view of the world and how we perceive ourselves in relation to others, which impacts the quality of the relationships we build. This in turn determines how empowering our relationships are to both ourselves and others, and how good we feel too.

When we are born, we are untainted by experience and possess a sense that all is OK. If we receive the love and attention we need to grow and thrive, then we get a sense that others around us are also OK. But then something happens.

---

9   Harris, TA (1973) *I'm OK – You're OK: Climb out of the cellar of your mind.* London: Random House

For example, despite getting an A in my exam, I'm told by my parents that nothing but an A+ will do. I then experience not being OK in relation to my parents, who are OK. If my best friend persistently breaks promises to me, I might decide that they are unreliable. They are not OK, while I am. Or I might find that everything seems to be going wrong at once, I can't rely on anyone and it's all my fault, so no one is OK. These experiences create filters for how I look at the world and feel good, or not so good, about myself and others.

The term OK is used to represent the feeling. This is represented in the quadrant in the illustration:

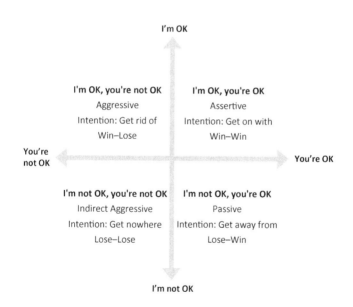

Common Life Positions. Adapted from: Stuart, I and Joines, V (1993) *TA Today: A new introduction to transactional analysis.* Nottingham: Lifespace Publishing, p120

I'm OK, you're OK

When I enter a situation or build a relationship from a place where I am OK and everyone else is too, I respect and appreciate both myself and others. This frees me up to be comfortable with other people, despite the fact that we may have differences, and I will be happy to work with them to get on with whatever we need to do. I am able to recognise my views and needs and ask for them to be met, and hear the views and needs of others. Working together, we find a solution that meets everyone's needs.

For example, say I need to introduce a change. The change itself has to happen and is non-negotiable, but how it happens is up to me. I ensure people are on board and engaged with it by respecting their needs and suggestions, taking time to understand their points of view.

I'm OK, you're not OK

When taking this life position, I will focus mainly on what I need, and will want others to go along with me with no regard for their perspectives. In actual fact, I find their perspectives rather a nuisance, not even worth considering. It's my way or the highway, and if they don't like it, then tough. I am not bothered by what they think or feel or the impact my actions and words will have on them because I don't respect them. Furthermore, I can't understand why anyone would resist my direction.

For example, a change in departmental structure is required. I decide who will be placed where and then tell everybody with the expectation that they will follow my commands.

I'm not OK, you're OK

When I'm in this position, I put myself and my needs below everyone else's. What they think and feel is more important than me; I don't respect my needs and my rights, and may not even recognise that I have any rights.

For example, in leading a change, I will listen to everyone and find out what they need. Then the change doesn't happen because everyone has so many competing needs and opinions, I cannot address them all. Their rights are more important than mine, so who am I to influence and negotiate?

I'm not OK, you're not OK

When in this position, we view the situation as a hopeless case. What is the point of me saying anything because people won't listen anyway? They are wrong and I am too useless to challenge them. I cannot express myself directly to them because I am not OK, and they don't express themselves directly to me because they're not able to do so.

For example, although I don't agree with the change, I don't voice my concerns directly. On the contrary, I agree publicly, and then carry on behaving as I was, and that undermines the change being implemented.

It is valuable to understand these four life positions. They help us recognise the different ways we might be approaching a situation and give us a frame of reference for identifying behaviours that work and those that don't. Aiming for a win-win and getting on with others is going to reap benefits in how we influence and engage. It doesn't mean we don't challenge others and voice our own views, but it does mean we respect and listen to others' views as well as our own and take them all into account.

Because of our life experiences, we have a tendency to find one element of the quadrant more comfortable than the others, and this is our default position. This doesn't mean we can't move around the quadrant, and indeed we normally do, depending on circumstances, but our default position is the one we go to unconsciously.

REALITY CHECK

In which I find myself in the 'I'm not OK, you're OK' position

I was selected to coach a leader who was the figurehead of large, well-known organisation. A highly intelligent man with a long, successful career behind him, he appeared frequently in the media, on both radio and TV.

My own default life position is I'm not OK, you're OK, so when I was initially selected by him, I was immediately consumed by concern and doubts. What would someone like me be able to offer this highly successful leader?

It wasn't until I talked it through with my coaching supervisor that I saw how the things I was making up about my new client's superiority to me were triggering an irrational ego reaction. That reaction wasn't in touch with the fact that my client had seen something in me that I could offer him.

Stepping back and reviewing how I had reacted helped me see clearly what I did have to offer. His experiences were different to my own, yet there were evidently areas of need that he had in relation to how he managed the challenges of his demanding role which I could help him with. This helped me shift my perspective to one of I'm OK, you're OK, which freed me up from the self-imposed constraints I was putting around the situation, enabling me to work with him effectively.

EXERCISE

Consider for yourself what your default life position may be and how this may help or hinder you.

- What are the short-term gains you get from this?

- And the long-term consequences?

Another way this model is valuable is in helping you develop a positive mindset.

REALITY CHECK

In which Louise manages some tricky behaviour with her line manager

Louise was navigating a tricky change. On top of that, she had a line manager who, although well intentioned, tended to speak out without giving any thought to the impact he was having. His 'fire, ready, aim' approach resulted in a lot of noses being put out of joint, and Louise had to dig deep to access her most effective influencing and diplomacy skills to keep the project on track.

What helped her was constantly reminding herself to take the position of I'm OK, you're OK and aim for a win-win. This even involved her taking time before important meetings to run the phrase 'I'm OK, you're OK' through her head like a mantra to support her to be at her most receptive and effective.

EXERCISE

Think of a relationship where you are resorting to an unhelpful life position. This could be in or outside of work.

- Which position are you adopting?

- What decisions have you made about yourself and the other person or people?

- On what basis have you made these?

- To what extent are they based on truth or assumption?

- What are you gaining from holding this position?

- What is the potential long term consequence of holding this position?

- What one or two things could you do to shift your perspective and bring this relationship into the position of I'm OK, you're OK?

Think of a relationship where you are resorting to an unhelpful position. What one or two things can you do to bring this relationship into a position of I'm OK, you're OK?

The roles our ego can take

The next model is designed to help us understand the different elements of ourselves and our personalities, and how they act out in relation to others. We are all born essentially OK, but as we experience life, things happen. We make decisions, we learn to act and be in certain ways that result in us being OK or not OK.

Transactional analysis (TA), developed by the psychiatrist Eric Berne,[10] is a long-established model that helps us go deeper into what goes on in relationships. Feedback from my clients tells me this is a highly valued model. It really helps us to understand more about what is going on for ourselves and in our interactions with others.

Berne was interested in how our personalities are formed and used 'parent', 'adult', and 'child' metaphorically as ways to illustrate the different aspects of our

---

10 Berne, E (1964) *Games People Play: The psychology of human relationships.* USA: Random House

personality and the impact they have. He described each element as an ego state, and as we grow and develop to adulthood, we develop our own unique balance of each.

Parent

From newborn into childhood, we soak up all the communication that is going on around us and develop a parent ego state that is full of parental messages.

Think about the style of communication that comes from parents. Think about your own parents or care givers, or how you are if you are a parent now. There are different qualities to the way a parent communicates – loving, caring, nurturing, but also setting limits and rules, and disciplining or punishing when these are broken. In soaking up this style of communication, we develop an ego state which is full of parental messages and ways of being.

What distinguishes this ego state from other aspects of our personality is that it is ruled by judgement. When coming from a parent ego state, we are extending power over others, as well as taking responsibility away from them. The illustration represents the parent ego state and its different elements and qualities.

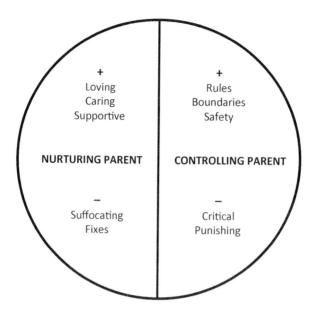

Parent ego state – ruled by judgement. Adapted from Stewart, I and Joines, V (1993) *TA Today: A new introduction to transactional analysis.* Lifespace Publishing, Nottingham, p21 and 25

When we're communicating from our parent ego state, our intention is to care, look after, love and keep safe, but this may not always play out in terms of how the interaction impacts the other person. Our messages from this ego state are loaded with commands, judgements, unconscious biases, our beliefs and values, all of which we consider to be right.

A controlling parent ego can be experienced as critical or punitive, which undermines engagement. For example, an exasperated manager calls a team member into their office, exclaiming, 'Yet again, you were late.

This is just not good enough, you have got to do better!' On the one hand, the manager has the right to address their team member's lateness, but it's how they deliver the message that makes the difference. Do they want their team member to be motivated and committed to turning around their performance, or do they want them to feel resentful and misunderstood?

When we're communicating from the nurturing parent ego state, we provide support, which is helpful particularly if someone is upset, but when overplayed, this state risks smothering and limiting growth in others.

EXERCISE

Consider these statements:

- You obviously haven't thought this one through

- You should be...

- You must...

- Let me sort this out for you

- I'll deal with it like I always end up doing

- Don't do that

- Do this

- These are the rules

- You know fine well this is not what I expect

- No need to worry, all will be well

- If only they'd listen to me

- Yet again, you've missed the deadline, it's just not good enough

How do these statements resonate with you? Can you recall times when you were on the receiving end of them or something similar? How did that impact you? How did you feel?

What about yourself and communication? Which statements have you found yourself utilising? When you were communicating this way, how did you feel? What did you get out of communicating this way? And longer term, what did it cost you?

Child

Another ego state Berne introduced is child. This part of ourselves consists of the natural drives and emotions we are born with, but it's also the part that has learned to adapt to other people. The child has developed survival strategies.

Think about how children communicate and interact with each other and with their parents. Young children are in the present, one minute unhappy, and the next ecstatic. They have a huge imagination and playfulness. Ever curious, young children are always asking 'Why?' from the point of view of wanting to learn. They can also be argumentative and resist what their parents are asking them to do, or go along with others, even if they may feel forced at the time.

What distinguishes our child ego state from the other ways of being is that this part of ourselves is ruled by our emotions and emotional needs. As with the parent ego state, we develop a child ego state that has different elements to it.

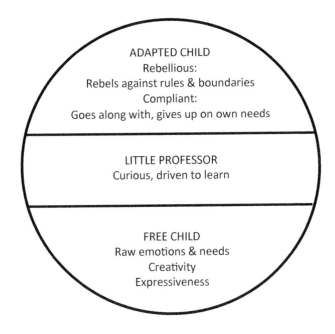

Child ego state – ruled by emotions and needs. Adapted from Stewart, I and Joines, V (1993) *TA Today, A new introduction to transactional analysis.* Lifespace Publishing, Nottingham, p21-24

Our child ego state can be broken down into three parts. Free child, the natural side of ourselves that expresses how we are feeling, be it love, anger, fear, happiness, is present in the moment, letting off steam and moving quickly on. This part of ourselves is highly creative and is a positive force in being able to inject energy and enthusiasm.

Then there is the part of our child ego that has learned to adapt to those around us, based on different types of fear. One fear is connected to our adapted child's need to be loved by those we regard as important to us, so to prevent rejection, we comply, often giving up on what we want and need. The other is the fear of being dominated, when what our adapted child strives for is independence and being in control, so we push against perceived rules and limits. This rebelliousness can be expressed overtly through angry and challenging be-haviour, or covertly through indirect expression such as agreeing with something to someone's face, but taking completely contrary action.

In life, we need a degree of compliance to make our world work. Imagine how hard life would be if there was only a tendency to rebel? What we don't need are people who consistently give up on what they need and don't challenge, because ultimately this leads to a lack of innovation. Similarly, pushing against rules and boundaries, breaking with convention, innovates and creates new ways of doing things. It's how we go about that rebellion that makes the difference. We need to learn to contain that part of ourselves so that we can influence positively.

There is a third innate part of the child ego state which is useful to us in all sorts of situations, in adulthood and as leaders as well as when we're growing up. This is the curious, questioning part of ourselves, known in Berne's model as the little professor. Curious about the world and our experiences within it, our active little professor will be keen to learn and understand why something is as it is, and supports us to seek out opportunities to grow and develop.

EXERCISE

Consider these statements:

- Loving life

- Let's go and...

- What if the worst happens?

- Do what you want

- No way

- You think you have problems, wait until you hear what happened to me

- Yes and...

- Imagine if...

- I don't care

- Please

- Fantastic new product

- Let's create...

- Why?

- No

- Yes

- Get lost!

- Am I bothered?

How do these statements resonate with you? Can you recall times when you were on the receiving end of them or something similar? How did that impact you? How did you feel?

What about yourself and communication? Which statements have you found yourself utilising? When you were communicating this way, how did you feel? What did you get out of communicating this way? And longer term, what did it cost you?

Adult

Adult is the third ego state described by Berne. The best way to think about this ego state is to reflect on what we mean when we say, 'Let's sit down and have an adult conversation about this'. What words come to mind? For me, they include mutual respect, calm, respectful, rational, based on facts and evidence, logical, unemotional, fair.

When using the parent ego state, we are interacting with the world from a set of rules and judgements that we decided on in our past. When we're in child state (with the exception of free child), we are also replaying learned behaviour from our past. Our adult ego state interacts in the present, free from past-based influences and using the facts and data we are currently faced with.

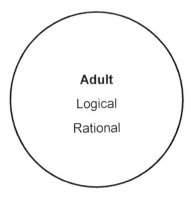

Adult ego state – ruled by facts and data in the here and now. Adapted from Stewart, I and Joines, V (1993) *TA Today: A new introduction to transactional analysis.* Lifespace Publishing, Nottingham, p21 and 26

Because adult is grounded in the present, we deal with the information we experience in the here and now. This information includes noticing the environment and atmosphere around us, other people's behaviour, our feelings and thoughts, and facts in relation to the task. When utilising the adult part of ourselves, we are able to focus on the facts and use them to help us navigate our conversations and circumstances, without being judgemental and emotional.

The downside of adult is that the logical, fact-based approach can be non-engaging. We human beings are emotional creatures, and it is engaging at an emotional level that enables us to feel connected.

Being adult is a great benefit to many important work conversations. When coming from this ego state, we are calm, open, able to listen and put our point of view across in a non-emotive or judgemental way. But staying purely in an adult state can mean we over focus on logic, which in situations such as team socials or creative thinking sessions can be counterproductive. In an emergency, parental judgement and command is vital.

Putting it all together

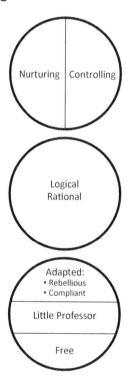

Putting it all together. Adapted from: Stuart, I and Joines, V (1993) *TA Today: A new introduction to transactional analysis*. Nottingham: Lifespace Publishing, p21–26

Consider all three ego states. They have their positives and they have their negatives too, illustrating the multifaceted elements of what it is to be human. We all have each ego state within us and play them out through our attitude and behaviour.

In an ideal world, adult would be in charge, logically selecting the most appropriate ego state for the circumstances we are faced with. But because of the human element, adult is not usually in charge. We are flitting between different egos, dependent on what we are reacting to at any given moment.

When we're leading others, whichever ego state we happen to be communicating from will impact those we are leading. Think about what it's like to be led by someone with a parent ego.

- What sort of things do they say and do?

- How do you feel when someone leads in this way?

- What are the short-term gains and long-term consequences?

Ask the same questions about what it's like to be led by someone who has a child ego state and what it's like being led by someone with an adult ego state.

How to navigate the different egos

Learn what triggers you

The challenge with applying parent/adult/child to ourselves and our relationships as leaders is that we often think we are being adult, when in actual fact we have slipped into a parent or child ego. That is because we get triggered by someone else's behaviour towards us and have a lack of awareness around our reactions. We may start with the clear intention of having an adult conversation or being more playful, but end up in a well-worn pattern of parental judgement or child-like compliance or rebellion.

For a large proportion of our daily lives, we are not conscious of our feelings, so they make themselves known to us when we have an emotional reaction. I call the stimulant that causes this sort of reaction a trigger – something that we react to emotionally in the moment when we see it as a perceived threat to ourselves, which then impacts how we are being.

Read some of the examples below:

- You are speeding on the motorway, and suddenly in your rear-view mirror, you see blue lights flashing. How do you feel? What do you do?

- After putting a lot of work into your report, your manager gives you only negative feedback. How do you feel? How do you behave?

- You arrive at an important meeting to find that for the umpteenth time, someone else has taken your pre-booked room. How do you feel? How do you respond?

- After a sleepless night and a workday full of challenges where everything appears to have gone wrong, a colleague reaches out and asks how you are. What do you feel? How do you respond?

Reviewing the above, you may have different intensities of reaction to each point, but it's worth considering what the trigger is any time you find yourself reacting and not being completely in control of your feelings and actions.

Triggers occur at three levels:

Ourselves. We may be triggered by our thoughts and how we relate to ourselves. For example, I was driving to deliver a workshop an hour away from my home and, almost at the venue, I suddenly thought I'd left all my notes and materials for the event back in my office. I immediately flushed, braked and pulled over, anxiously berating myself for being so forgetful. On checking the boot, I found everything was there. I had imagined it all and triggered myself.

Think about how you might cause yourself to react in an unhelpful way by criticising yourself or holding yourself back.

Others – both people and things. It's probably much easier to think about how other people or things trigger us than how we trigger ourselves. As human beings, we find it so easy to put the blame on to somebody else or our circumstances. It could be someone's tone of voice, their overall manner, or that they say the wrong thing at the wrong time.

System. Things that go on in the organisations in which we work can trigger us. My experience of the training room that I found incorrectly set up, which I shared in a reality check right at the beginning of the book, is an example.

The thing about triggers is they are based on our perceptions. They relate to our basic fight or flight instinct, so we react, but that reaction is not necessarily the most helpful response. For example, in my annoyance at my line manager's criticism of my report, I might sit quietly while they go through each point, but I've already decided they are wrong, so I am not really listening (rebel child reaction).

Another thing about triggers is that they are reactions based on either unconscious past-based decisions or future-focused anxiety. The flashing blue lights in the rear-view mirror cause me to put my foot on the brake because I am frightened that I will get a fine, points on my licence or even a driving ban – all worries about the future, stimulated by learning from the past.

My line manager's feedback and the tone they deliver it in (parent ego) remind me of being reprimanded at school and I respond accordingly in child ego. So, if I am coming from the past or concerned about the future, I am not present, and being present is one of the antidotes to being triggered.

When something triggers me and I unconsciously react, I experience a loss of power. I might feel powerful in the moment, but ultimately there will be an impact. For example, closing myself off to my line manager's feedback blocks off my ability to learn and may ultimately jeopardise how my line manager views my attitude and performance. If I am present and not replaying decisions or experiences from the past, or present and not feeling anxious or concerned about the future, I am in a better place to choose how I respond. Responding is different to reacting in that it comes from a place of conscious choice. Being present to and recognising my emotions, I can use them as valuable information to guide how I respond.

For example, noticing my line manager's tone and perceiving the criticism they have about my report, I feel annoyed. But rather than acting on that annoyance, I can choose to simply notice it and let it pass before responding to my line manager in a more open and curious way.

Why are we vulnerable to being triggered? There are a variety of circumstances that might result in us being triggered, for example:

- When we are unaware of our emotions and the impact they have on both ourselves and others

- When we have a lot on our plate, too many things to think about, so we are less able to be conscious and manage ourselves and our responses

- Tiredness

- For women, time of the month

- Something happened earlier that is impacting our state, eg we've received bad news

- A decision we've made in the past, based on an impactful experience in our childhood and now influencing us from our unconscious

- Our preferred ego traps, which guide what we filter for.

I'm sure you can add examples of your own. Whatever causes you to be vulnerable to being triggered, developing awareness around it gives you a chance to do something about it.

It can help to understand the process we go through. Here's what tends to happen, consciously or unconsciously.

Something happens – trigger
(example: my boss's tone)

Emotional reaction – I feel annoyed

Thought – how dare they?

Decision – I am not going along with this

Action – I sit silently and resentfully in the meeting

Impact – on self? On others?

Consider what you are getting out of your reaction. Is there short-term gain, for example you feel self-righteous? Take a look and tell the truth to yourself.

As human beings, we don't do anything unless we are getting something from it, even when we take a position that might not on the surface appear that pleasant (eg annoyed, miserable, indignant). Returning to my annoyance with my boss, I am triggered because I feel vulnerable, so when my boss criticises me, my resentful behaviour is a defence against my vulnerability being exposed. It is safer to take a position of counterattack and reject my boss's comments, justifying this to myself by seeing my boss as a negative person.

Ever heard of the term 'self-imposed psychic prison'? This is exactly what we do: we trap ourselves through our own viewpoints, decisions and assumptions, and because we are triggered, often outside of our conscious awareness, we can get stuck in these viewpoints. We then get a great deal of satisfaction out of being self-righteous about our point of view and look for further evidence that backs it up, resisting evidence that might point to the contrary.

Long-term consequences

We can get stuck in our reaction because we are getting something out of it immediately, but there are long-term consequences.

Back to the criticising boss scenario. I am indignant and resistant to what they are saying, so in our conversation I am not really open to any contribution. I am preserving my fragile ego, but I have shut myself off to the learning opportunity.

Think about what the long-term consequences of my behaviour and attitude may be. I don't develop or build self-awareness, which stops me from being able to see my strengths and capabilities, and my report writing certainly won't improve. My relationship with my boss suffers, reducing trust and connection, so my reaction has a negative impact on others. I become perceived as someone who is closed or a moaner.

Staying stuck with my point of view, I lose personal power, which impacts on my results – I don't achieve what I want. Ultimately, this impacts on my career when I don't get the promotions I want.

Whenever you get stuck in your own position and are making other people wrong, you are potentially losing power. You may feel fine in the moment, but you won't longer term. So, can you avoid being triggered?

We are always going to be vulnerable to reacting, but there are many things we can do to help us be more conscious of ourselves and increase our resilience. Becoming familiar with our feelings and what they are informing us of, rather than reacting to them, is certainly helpful. Keeping a log of our emotions and the triggers we experience during any given day allows us to see where our trigger points are. Strengthening our personal foundation, including our integrity, health and wellbeing, contributes to a more positive sense of self, which contributes to us having greater self-esteem, which in turn helps us either not be triggered in the first place, or manage ourselves more effectively when we are.

Understanding more about the nuances of human behaviour and what goes on in relationships can also help. For example, back in the reality check in Chapter 1, Jennifer offered feedback to her boss and he rejected and challenged her. She immediately reverted to being compliant and worried about her job security. The way Jennifer's boss responded to her triggered an anxiety that resulted in her unconsciously reacting to him from the ego state of compliant child.

This reality check also illustrates how Jennifer's boss' ego was triggered. He hadn't asked for her feedback and may well have felt exposed or vulnerable when she gave it. Therefore, he defended himself from the controlling parent ego state. Both Jennifer and John had the intention of being calm, rational and reasonable, but they fell into communicating from their default child or parent egos.

EXERCISE

Select a day to do this. Over the course of the day, keep a log of when you recognise yourself being triggered into parent or child ego states.

- Describe the scenario. Who did it involve?

- What was the actual trigger? Tone of voice?
  The person you were dealing with? The words on an email? A problem of some sort?

- What was the underlying concern, thought or feeling you experienced?

- What meaning did you attribute to this?

- How did you then react?

Log several trigger times over the course of the day. Review – look at what you have written up and notice:

- Any themes that are coming through for you.

- When are you most vulnerable?

- Which ego state do you tend to slip into when triggered?

How our ego states can contaminate our thinking

The purpose of TA is to help us understand ourselves and our interactions with others better so that we can restore and maintain our sense of OK-ness. Yet the development of our ego states is not neat and tidy. We have experiences where we internalise beliefs, making decisions about ourselves, others and the world that distort how we view logical reality. Our parent and child invade the boundaries of adult, and our rational adult ego accepts as true what actually are distortions of reality. Using Berne's language, this merging is known as contamination, because we are no longer communicating from purely one ego state.[11]

---

11   Stuart, I and Joines, V (1993) *TA Today: A new introduction to transactional analysis*. Nottingham. Lifespace Publishing, p50-51

Parent contamination

This refers to taught beliefs, often prejudices that are expressed as facts. The language a person coming from this ego state uses is generalised, often put into second or third person and expressed as a fact, even though they are talking about themselves. For example: 'People find it really hard to change'; 'You just can't trust people'; 'All our leaders are out of touch'. Contamination can impact large segments of society, even causing changes in the law. Another example of a generalised view is that of immigration as the cause of job losses and a downturn in the economy.

In organisational terms, parental contamination impacts the cultural beliefs and prejudices that hold limiting elements of the system in place, such as the challenge in achieving gender balance, or the lack of balance between focus on results and the engagement of people to achieve the results.

EXERCISE

- Take two minutes to write down all the slogans and beliefs you hear in your organisation.

- Review these and check whether each one is an actual statement of reality or a parent contamination.

Child contamination

When in the child contamination state, we allow our adult thinking to be clouded by past beliefs and experiences from childhood. These are actually fantasies evoked by our emotions, for example 'People don't like me'; 'I'm invincible'; 'I don't have what it takes', that we take as facts, resulting in us becoming deluded.

Within organisations, certain ways of being come through child contamination, for example 'Our leaders need big elbows to succeed'; 'We are the greatest organisation in the world'.

EXERCISE

Write down as many endings to the following sentence as you think apply to you:

- I am the sort of person who...

After a couple of minutes, sit back, relax and take a look at what you have written. For each statement, check whether it is based in reality or something that you are carrying from your childhood.

Contamination occurs when we get hooked or triggered by a situation or someone else's behaviour and our reaction is based on unconscious beliefs and thoughts.

Clearing up contamination

What enables us to reduce contamination in ourselves is the ongoing journey of self-awareness, plus questions we can ask of ourselves and others when we perceive their reality is being affected by contamination.

Example of contaminated statement	Grounding questions
'People find it really hard to change.'	Which people?
	Do you mean everyone?
	What makes it hard?
'You can't trust people.'	Do you mean never ever?
	How can you start to trust them?
	When have you trusted someone?
'You've just got to stay positive.'	Is that always the case?
	What would help with that?
'My face doesn't fit here.'	How do you know?
	What evidence is there for that?
'I will make it happen!'	How do you mean?
'I don't have what it takes.'	What specifically are you referring to?

Consider where your own thoughts or communication may be contaminated and use questions like the ones I've listed to help you develop a clearer view of reality.

Our internal dialogue

It is also important to be aware of how we relate to ourselves. What is the nature and tone of our internal dialogue? Do we have an internal voice that is critical or nurturing?

My experience is most people have a highly developed internal critical parent. Even the most experienced CEO can be the hardest judge on themselves. You may give yourself a hard time when things don't go well or undermine your self-belief when you're nervous about a new challenge you are taking on. Take the time to notice how you react to these circumstances. Engage with being more nurturing and compassionate with yourself; you're likely to be surprised how this in itself can reduce your sense of stress and overwhelm.

Summary

This chapter has introduced two models that help you explore what underpins the way you communicate and build relationships. Exploring your internal processes and having a framework from which to understand them can give you access to being more aware of yourself and put you in a powerful place of choosing how you respond.

I recommend you revisit this chapter to support you on your journey. Consider the different ways you may be empowering or limiting yourself, moving towards a more integrated and adult approach when you need to.

REFLECTION

Think about the different models we've explored:

- Which elements resonated most with you?

- Why do you think that was?

- How could you apply these frameworks to help you as a leader?

6
Dynamics Of Our Relationships With Others

We'll explore:

- Interpersonal transactions
- Psychological games
- How to spot a game
- Addressing games

L eading is a relational act. We cannot do it without connecting with others, and what causes that connection is the quality of our listening and our presence when we're in conversation with others.

It's worth considering a bit more about what goes on when we are communicating and relating to others so that we can build relationships that really engage. We need to develop the ability to navigate the interactions and dynamics not only in our personal communications and relationships, but also across the organisations in which we work.

In the previous chapter, we looked at the difference our life position makes and how the view we hold of ourselves and other people affects the way we engage with them. We unpacked the different elements of our ego and how these impact the quality of our interpersonal communication. We're now going to explore what happens when we interact with others further.

Interpersonal transactions

When one person says something, it leads to a response. The other person says or does something in return. Berne calls these interactions 'transactions', and they are initiated by a stimulus.

Parallel transactions

These interactions are mutual and complementary. On the whole, both participants are coming from the same ego states in the transaction. For example:

Parent to parent, the gossiping when two people in critical parent ego states are having a chat

Stimulus: 'There's going to be another restructure, seems to me that the powers that be have no idea what they are doing.'

Response: 'You're right, and the money they must be wasting is scandalous.'

Adult to adult, the logical and factual conversation between two people being adult

Stimulus: 'What time are we meeting today?'

Response: 'I have it scheduled for 3.30pm.'

Child to child, the emotional expressiveness of two people coming from free child states

Stimulus: 'Let's play with some ideas for how we can improve this.'

Response: 'I would love to do that.'

All these interactions are complementary and each participant is happy, getting their needs met. Parallel transactions are considered normal healthy human communication and will usually continue quite smoothly. There is one more transaction that is considered parallel and that is between parent and child ego states. For example:

Stimulus: 'I've had a really tough day' – child ego state appealing to parent.

Response: 'Never mind, tomorrow will be better, I'm sure' – nurturing parent appealing to child.

While this style of transaction is supportive and nurturing, which is positive in the short term, it doesn't necessarily help people to grow. On the contrary, in fact, it can result in over-dependence on the leader being able to find the solution and fix the problem. While transactions remain parallel and complementary, communication continues to run smoothly and can do so indefinitely. But what happens when transactions become crossed?

Crossed transactions

When a transaction is crossed, it means that the ego state being addressed in the initial stimulus is not the one that responds, so the response is unexpected. For example:

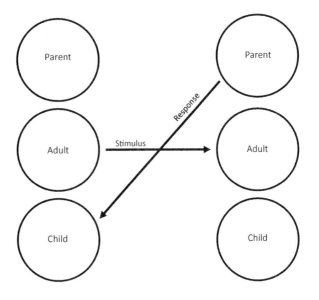

Example of a crossed transaction – Adult-Adult stimulus, Parent-Child response. Adapted from: Stuart, I and Joines, V (1993) *TA Today: A new introduction to transactional analysis*. Nottingham: Lifespace Publishing, p63

Adult-to-adult stimulus, parent-to-child response

Stimulus: Adult to Adult: 'I've mislaid the most recent report; could you resend it, please?'

Response: Parent to Child: 'You really need to be more organised.'

What do you think the response of the first person might be? They could restore the parallel communication by responding from a child state, for example apologising and complying by agreeing, or rebelling by disagreeing. Either way, when a transaction is crossed, it hinders and can even stop the progress of the communication as the point of the communication is lost. In this example, there is a risk that the report won't be resent.

Ulterior transactions

As the name suggests, an ulterior transaction describes communication that goes on at two levels. On the surface or social level, we're conveying one message overtly, but underneath, at the psychological level, there is a hidden covert message. The overt message is usually adult to adult, the covert message generally parent to child or child to parent. What happens is that the covert psychological message is frequently the one that the other person picks up on. When we're on the receiving end, we may well end up feeling like we have been manipulated.

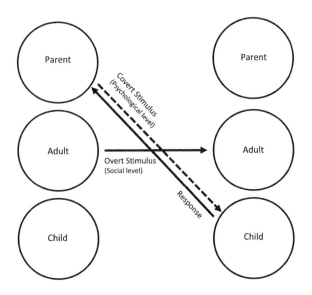

Example of an ulterior transaction – Overt Adult-Adult stimulus, covert Parent-Child stimulus. Adapted from Stuart, I and Joines, V (1993) *TA Today: A new introduction to transactional analysis*. Nottingham: Lifespace Publishing, p239 and p242

Ulterior transaction – overt adult to adult, covert parent to child

Stimulus: Adult with ulterior Controlling Parent: 'From what you've told me, this car is out of your price range.'

Response: Adapted (rebellious) Child: 'Nonsense, I'll take it.'

This classic car salesperson example demonstrates how manipulative ulterior transactions have the potential to be.

In summary, when leading and managing others, we need to be aiming to engage in parallel transactions which support the flow of helpful communication. When we're in these interactions, our communication is authentic and we and the other person are both OK. On the other hand, we need to be mindful of our use of inauthentic crossed or ulterior transactions. These have the potential to cause communication breakdown and risk disengagement and disconnection with those we are leading.

EXERCISE

- Reflect on the interactions you have with others.

- Write down an example of each type of transaction you experience.

- What is the impact of each?

Psychological games

In reviewing your interactions in the exercise, did you spot any where you came away feeling not OK? Can you think of other times you've been in an interaction and come away feeling not OK about it? Or where you might have felt self-righteous and OK, but the other person wasn't?

Sometimes, the interactions we get into result in confusion and a familiar but powerless experience. We might even find ourselves saying, 'I can't believe what just happened' or 'Why does this keep happening to me?' When this happens, the chance is that we are involved in a psychological game.

Games are going on all over the place. In fact, Eric Berne said, 'Do not ask whether you are playing a game, ask which game you are playing.'[12]

If we can become aware of the unhelpful games we are involved in, we have a greater chance of addressing them and moving towards more connected relationships with others.

The Drama Triangle

A helpful model to explore in relation to games is the Drama Triangle created by Stephen Karpman. The Drama Triangle is aptly named because it refers to the dramas we can create in our relationships and communications with others.

Karpman describes three roles we get into. These roles are interchangeable and we dance around them in our interactions with others.

---

12   Stuart, I and Joines, V (1993) *TA Today: A new introduction to transactional analysis*. Nottingham. Lifespace Publishing, p241-242

The Drama Triangle. Source: Karpman, SB (2014) *A Game Free Life: The definitive book on the Drama Triangle and Compassion Triangle by the originator and author.* Drama Triangle Publications. Figure used with kind permission of Dr Stephen Karpman MD.

- **Persecutor** – when in this role, we are coming from our Controlling Parent ego and tend to be judgemental, critical, unsympathetic and even punitive – 'I'm OK, you're not OK.'

- **Rescuer** comes from Nurturing Parent. While we're communicating in a more sympathetic way than the persecutor, we still take over, fixing things and disrespecting the capability of the other person – 'I'm OK, you're not OK.'

- **Victim** – when we are in this role, we are coming from the Child ego. We feel powerless, put upon, life's unfair, we blame and avoid responsibility – 'I'm not OK, you're OK.'

REALITY CHECK

In which Dave and his line manager Janine slip into a game

Victim: Dave comes to Janine for some help. He is fed up because he can't see himself getting away by five to attend his son's school play that evening.

Rescuer: Janine is concerned for Dave, but also tired of his constant moaning. Although feeling slightly resentful, she feels duty bound to support him, so she listens while he lists a whole host of things that reinforce his powerless victim status. Janine makes suggestions, but Dave has a reason as to why each one would never work.

'Yes, I could do that, but...' he says repeatedly.

After some time, Janine feels herself getting increasingly impatient, and when Dave says, 'Yes, but...' again, she is suddenly triggered.

Persecutor: Janine's voice rises in pitch and she exclaims, 'You're completely closed off to any advice! You're just going to have to sort it out yourself!' It's like a switch has clicked and Janine snaps into persecutor. This ultimately reinforces Dave's life position that he can't be helped (I'm not OK) and everything is useless (you're not OK), and results in him feeling bad about himself and the world generally. Janine also feels bad about herself as she hasn't behaved according to her view of how a good leader 'should' behave.

What Dave is doing on the social level is asking for help, but on the psychological level he is proving that he cannot be helped. Janine on the social level is

> responding to him as she believes a good leader should, when psychologically she is feeling tired of Dave's complaining and lack of responsibility. Janine puts on a good front of caring, while Dave resists any sort of solution so he can stay in his disempowered place. Eventually, Janine snaps and behaves like the autocratic leader she doesn't want to be.

How to spot a game

Game dynamics go on in relationships all over the place. We flit in and out of the different roles unconsciously. Organisations are no different, with games going on between individuals, teams and departments. For example, in one organisation I worked with, Marketing repeatedly criticised Operations' inability to deliver on the level of service promised in the brochure (persecutor to victim), or in another, a local council, Children's Services complained they felt like a football (victim), kicked around between finance and the councillors (persecutors) and invited an external agency to come in and sort out some issues (rescuer).

If psychological games go on unconsciously, how do we know when we are getting into one? Fortunately, there are ways to identify this. Here are some signs of a game.

1. There is a series of ulterior transactions. In other words, there is inconsistency between what is

being said and the message going on underneath. For example: 'That's great news, your team did so well, and aren't you lucky to have inherited such a strong team in the first place?' Overt message – 'Well done, congratulations.' Covert message – 'You didn't do it, your team did. You're not capable.'

This can be subtle, communicated via tone of voice or body language alone. For example, different inflections on the way we say, 'Well done' can communicate numerous different meanings. The thing about our non-verbal messages is that they often leak what we are really thinking and are easily picked up by the receiver.

2. There is a repetitive pattern of behaviour and interaction in your relationships. For example, are you always fighting someone else's corner for them or working really hard and then being overlooked? Does the interaction in a certain relationship have an inevitable outcome? Is it getting predictable? You may think, 'Here we go again', and even though you see the conversation going in a direction you don't like, it's difficult to do something to stop it. Despite the inauthenticity, both parties are getting something out of the interaction, perhaps being seen to be doing the right thing. In other words, some need is getting met, albeit in an unhelpful way.

3. There is a switch where the roles in the transaction suddenly change, resulting in one or both parties being psychologically put down. They experience a loss of personal power and a negative feeling – in Karpman's terms, this is known as a 'psychological kick'. For example, you may be lost for words, feel annoyed and react angrily or accusatorily, be confused, or find yourself agreeing while unclear on what you are agreeing to. The pay-off proves your default ego state is right, hence the sense of familiarity.

It can be hard to admit that we get into any of the roles in the Drama Triangle, but if we want to create relationships where we and the other person both feel OK and maintain a sense of personal power and responsibility, we need to be honest with ourselves and own up to the different positions we can get into. Fortunately, by being aware, we can choose what we do and how we behave.

Addressing games

Once we are aware of the games, we can shift the roles we are playing and adopt more positive ones. This is when getting in touch with our adult state comes into its own. But skilfully managing the dynamics and roles that go on within the Drama Triangle requires not just a logical approach, but also the ability to be in touch with our emotions from the child part of us and clear boundaries and limits from the parent part. Increased levels of self-awareness, as well as our ability to tune in to what is actually going on in the drama and access what both we and others really need, enable us to shift into different ways of being that ensure we are OK and so is the other person.

This is represented by the Authentic Triangle.[13]

Authentic Triangle

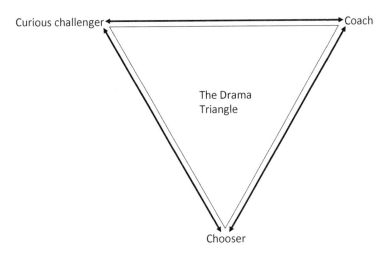

The Authentic Triangle. Adapted from: Karpman, SB (2014) *A Game Free Life: The definitive book on the Drama Triangle and Compassion Triangle by the originator and author.* Drama Triangle Publications

13 Original concept by Dr Stephen Karpman MD. Variation is the author's own, by kind permission of Dr Karpman.

Curious challenger replaces persecutor

Rather than being annoyed and critical when challenging someone, we can assert our observations of the situation without being punitive.

To get access to a different way of being that will shift us out of I'm OK, you're not OK behaviour, we need to look beyond the actual behaviour and its impact to the intention behind the behaviour. On the surface, the persecutor lands a punitive message, eg 'You're completely closed off to any advice', but underneath is a different intention, one of concern – of wanting the victim to open up, to learn, to challenge a perceived limitation.

Challenging is absolutely valid and necessary to enable high performance. But it's how we challenge that will make the difference as to whether we persist in the Drama Triangle or break free of it. One way is to challenge from a place of being curious. This means letting go of having power over someone else and being right while making the other person wrong, and getting in touch with the free child in us who is motivated to learn and understand the world. When we do this, our challenge takes on a completely different tone. If we can understand what it is we really want or need for ourselves and the other person, then we can challenge from a place of positive intention.

Here are some examples of how we can turn judgemental persecutory statements into ones that still challenge, but do so from a place of curiosity.

> *Persecutor*: 'You're completely closed off to any advice, you're just going to have to sort it yourself.'

> *Curious challenger*: 'I'm noticing that we've discussed a few solutions and none of them appear to work for you. What's the best way for me to support you here?'

> *Persecutor*: 'You haven't hit your targets, it's just not good enough!'

> *Curious challenger:* 'I'm wondering what's going on that has resulted in your targets being missed.'

> *Persecutor*: 'I'm not prepared to be the nice guy anymore. You just don't get what it takes to step up, despite my constantly telling you.'

> *Curious challenger*: 'I need us as a team to step up and be more strategic. What is getting in the way that stops us progressing?'

Consider your own situations and note down some examples of the persecutor, and then turn them around to curious challenger.

Coach replaces rescuer

If we are prone to rescuing, it can be a hard behaviour to catch ourselves doing, mainly because, a bit like persecutor, we are coming from a place of being right. We may feel validated by having a genuine solution that makes us feel powerful. Someone has a need for support and help, and we have the answer, so we may feel it would be wrong not to offer it. But it's not helpful because it perpetuates the game. In rescuing the victim, we are not enabling them to learn and do things for themselves.

We can also become attached to being the one who has the right answer or knows the correct solution. As busy leaders, we may believe that offering this answer and dealing with the problem in the short term is the most reliable option, but in the long term, our people won't develop the capability we need. Instead, they will become overly reliant on us, and we will end up with far too much to do, keeping us in the detail rather than being more strategic.

To move from rescuer to coach takes a shift in mindset:

- **Trust** – that others have the resources they need to find their own solutions

- **Curiosity** – being curious takes us from the 'I know' persecutor mindset to opening up to possibilities

- **Belief in the resources of the other person** – recognising that others are capable and, when given the right support, can work things out and develop from the experience

Where a rescuer will fix, a coach will ask questions, be present, listen, observe, give feedback and challenge. For example:

Director: 'I need your help in sorting out a mess.'

Rescuer: 'Tell me what's happened.'

Director: 'I sent an email out to all senior leaders advising them of the changes we are making to their car parking arrangements, and every single one of them has come back, objecting and saying why it won't work.'

Rescuer: 'OK, how about you speak to each of them and get to the root of their concerns.'

Compare that to:

Director: 'I need your help in sorting out a mess.'

Coach: 'Tell me what's happened.'

Director: 'I sent an email out to all senior leaders advising them of the changes we are making to their car parking arrangements, and every single one of them has come back, objecting and saying why it won't work.'

Coach: 'OK. What do you believe is behind their lack of engagement?'

Chooser replaces victim

To move out of victim, we need to reclaim some personal power and choose a different response. The thing about being the victim is we don't feel we have any power, and can feel overwhelmed, even paralysed, by our circumstances. This is particularly true when we are experiencing the other person as highly persecutory. Another thing about being in victim – and this can keep us stuck here because it's something we get out of it – is that we are not taking responsibility.

To move from victim to chooser, we need to recognise what we can be responsible for and make some choices for ourselves. In that way, we open possibilities for action. This can happen in the most minute way, but as soon as we start to recognise we have a choice and can take action, we take back our power and potentially transform a situation.

REALITY CHECK

In which Julie catches herself getting caught in a game and gets herself out of it

Julie was a participant on one of my leadership development programmes supporting a change in culture. When she was in an important meeting with a more senior leader, he began to raise his voice and become quite derogatory and dismissive in his tone towards her. Julie felt uncomfortable, finding this behaviour difficult to deal with.

Previously she would have tolerated this and probably left the meeting feeling pretty bad. On this occasion, she recalled the Drama Triangle and, with an increased awareness of how things could go, recognised her discomfort of moving into victim mode.

She took a deep breath and chose to address what was happening, saying, 'I'm not sure what's going on here, but I am beginning to feel really uncomfortable in this conversation. There is something about your tone of voice and manner that I am finding difficult and I'm not prepared to continue this meeting if it goes on like this.'

The senior manager stopped short, completely taken aback by Julie's response. They agreed to stop the meeting so both could step back from it, and then reschedule.

When they met again, the senior leader apologised to Julie. He'd had no idea how his behaviour was impacting on her (or others, for that matter) and thanked her for her honest feedback. Their relationship transformed.

What Julie did in this situation was:

- Notice she was losing her power

- Recognise what was contributing to this

- Engage her adult ego

- Name the experience – Julie stated she was feeling uncomfortable and that this appeared to be to do with the senior manager's behaviour

- Choose to give feedback and make a request for change

She used her adult ego to communicate what wasn't working in a calm, fact-based way, taking on board her feelings which came from her child ego. She then brought in parent to set a boundary and state what she intended to do. Julie did not judge and make her colleague wrong; she kept to what was working and not working for her. In so doing, she reclaimed her personal power.

Many clients ask me what they can do in the moment to stop themselves falling into the trap of games. Below is a list of things that will definitely help:

- **Notice** – the key is to recognise what is happening, your experience and how you are feeling.

- **Breathe** – taking a moment to breathe in and out slowly sends oxygen to the brain and allows you

to change your state, transcend your ego
and engage a different part of yourself.
This is powerful.

- **Name the behaviour/experience** – share your
observations of what is happening.

- **Use responsible language** – own the experience
as yours using words such as 'I am noticing' or
'I am feeling'.

- **Call a halt** – if things are getting too out of
control, then stop the interaction to allow things
to cool down.

Summary

Relationship and communication games are going
on all the time. It's the ones that lead to negative ego
patterns and results that we need to be mindful of
and endeavour to manage differently; the ones that
risk non-engagement and people feeling angry, disillusioned and upset.

There are ways to manage games, but it takes conscious
effort. By being more aware of ourselves and what
is going on around us, we can respond differently
and communicate in an adult-centred way that con-
structively addresses the challenges we face in our
relationships with others.

REFLECTION

Think about a relationship or interaction that didn't go as well as you'd have liked.

- What game might have been going on?

Use the Drama Triangle structure to help you understand:

- What different roles did you and the other person go through?

- How can you address this interaction?

Use the Authentic Triangle to help you address how this interaction plays out.

7
Developing Our Adult Ego

We'll explore:

- Why an adult approach is effective
- Building a strong personal foundation
- Self-awareness and self-belief
- The importance of purpose

The challenge of leading in the new normal is that it can trigger ego-driven reactions, resulting in critical, controlling, rebellious or submissive behaviour in both ourselves and others. Taking people with you as you lead change requires navigation of not only many different circumstances, but also many different egos, including your own as the leader.

One of the key features of an effective leader in these times of uncertainty is the need for calmness and transparency.[14] This takes a high degree of self-awareness

---

14 Johansen, R (2012) *Leaders Make the Future: Ten new leadership skills for an uncertain world.* San Francisco: Berrett-Koehler

and self-management of your inner child, which is where your emotions are triggered, and your controlling parent, the part that may want to take over and fix everything to help alleviate your anxiety.

What can you put in place to support you to manage your anxiety, stay calm and grounded, and effectively lead others through uncertainty? The answer is the development of the adult ego. That doesn't mean excluding your feelings and emotions (child), or your ability to set expectations and boundaries (parent). When navigating uncertainty, being able to tune into and communicate our feelings and expectations in a calm, rational, yet empathetic way is both powerful and empowering. I call this 'integrated adult'. This is when our 'adult' is in control, accessing our feelings and judgement to communicate authentically.

Why is an adult approach effective?

Each ego state possesses positives and negatives. Adult is not without its foibles. For example, on a team night out, where the invitation is to let your hair down and express yourself from free child, a leader relating from a purely adult ego would be regarded as rather boring and disengaging.

The truth is that what really engages us is our emotions. Look at the way TV reality shows present their contestants' stories. Homing in on the tragedy or the hard-fought battle of the contestants, they use emotions as a hook to get us watching the whole series. Similarly, the rules and boundaries generated through our parent ego state are helpful in creating safety and clarity, which influences how much people are able to be themselves and feel trusted and trusting. But developing our adult will give us access to getting in touch with our parent and child so we can share how we are feeling responsibly, making requests and agreements with others which promote engagement and trust.

Adult with an integration of child and parent keeps the drama at bay through:

a. being sensitive to feelings and using them as information to help us identify our needs.

b. setting boundaries that support effective working and dealing with challenging conversations.

Build a strong personal foundation

Look at an everyday activity, such as driving your car. How does your performance compare between driving the day after a really late night, where you didn't get much sleep, and a day where you are feeling fully refreshed and alert? This simple scenario illustrates how your performance can vary based on your level of resources at the time, in this case sleep. If you are starting your day early, finishing late, not taking proper breaks, not eating properly or having time to have fun with your friends and family, your personal energy resources will be depleted, impacting your resilience and ability to be present and conscious to managing yourself and your thoughts and emotions. Just like driving the car, you are going to find it far more difficult to be adult when you are tired and stressed than when you are energised and healthy.

This is why strengthening your personal foundation is so valuable. It puts you in a place to be the best you can be with optimum energy, physically, mentally and emotionally, which increases your ability to be present and aware, able to monitor your reactions and appreciate with clarity what is going on around you.

Creating a strong personal foundation means putting things in place that support you to be your best, present, centred and grounded. What this foundation provides you with is the ability to make decisions and take actions from a place of understanding about what is (adult), which increases options and choices. Without this, you are vulnerable to reacting blindly without conscious awareness, impacting the results you achieve.

A strong personal foundation also supports your well-being and resilience when you're leading through constant change and needing to take others with you.

A holistic approach

When addressing your personal foundation, you need to consider the whole of yourself, not just one specific element. It's not only about being physically fit, but also about your mental, emotional and spiritual wellbeing. Leading in volatile times requires you to be mentally alert, emotionally in tune with yourself and others, and able to connect to the bigger system.

As individuals, we have many different aspects to our lives, and how one part of our life is going impacts the others. In strengthening our foundation, we need to look beyond our working circumstances to how our personal lives are supporting us.

Sports psychologist, Jim Loehr and journalist Tony Schwartz knew all about what created high performance in athletes and trained some of the best. But they were increasingly called upon by the corporate world to look at how they could apply some of their thinking and methods to optimise executive performance. In their book *The Power Of Full Engagement* they noticed the demands and regimes differed between athletes and executives.

	Athlete	Executive
Regime	Bespoke diet geared to optimum nutrition and health	No special diet, limited breaks
Training	Specialist focused training around specific sport	Generalised training
Recovery and recuperation	Regular and prolonged periods of rest between competitions	Long hours with 24-hour availability through technology
	Seasonal activity often with three to four months off per year	Short periods of rest and holidays four times a year
Career lifespan	Short, often retiring in their thirties	Career trajectory can be over forty to fifty years

Details shared with kind permission of Jim Loehr and Tony Schwartz[15]

Loehr and Schwartz make some useful distinctions from their sports coaching that can be applied to the world of work to support executives to be their best.

Distinction 1: Energy not time is the currency of high performance and full engagement. Time is finite; there are only so many hours in a day and we cannot make any difference to that. Energy is a personal resource that we do have some control over. We can look at what drains us and what gives us energy, make choices and take action to ensure our energy is at an optimum.

---

15   Loehr, J and Schwartz, T (2005) *The Power Of Full Engagement: Managing energy, not time, is the key to high performance and personal renewal*. New York: The Free Press

It is, after all, the energy we put into something that will affect the quality of attention we give to it.

Distinction 2: Break the working day into a series of short sprints rather than treating it like a marathon. This means breaking our day down into activities that have a clear start and finish point, and between each activity doing something to recover and top up our energy.

That break doesn't have to be long; it can simply mean getting up from our desk and walking around the building or going to the kitchen to get a drink, but it does involve moving around and allowing ourselves a short period of recuperation before we move on to our next activity. This approach encourages us to keep our energy resources topped up, supporting our ability to concentrate, be present and respond from our adult ego state.

Distinction 3: Look after the whole of ourselves. When we think of energy, we automatically tend to think of being physically energetic. Loehr and Schwartz describe our physical energy as our foundation which supports all other types of energy.

They then describe three other types of energy:

- **Mental energy** - our ability to intellectually focus and shift between the small detail and the bigger picture

- **Emotional energy** - our ability to relate to others and create mutually loving and supportive relationships

- **Spiritual energy** - our ability to connect to the bigger system of our world and nature (note this is not necessarily spirituality linked to religion.)

Distinction 4: Rituals and routines keep our energy topped up. A ritual or routine is something we do automatically without even thinking. For example, when we get up in the morning, we get washed and clean our teeth, probably putting little thought into it. We run this routine on automatic pilot. But have you ever left the house and realised you haven't cleaned your teeth? It feels yucky, and on a microscopic level may impact your comfort for the day, which affects your energy. Rituals and routines help us put activities in place which ultimately support us in keeping our energy levels topped up.

I liken the four energies – physical, mental, emotional and spiritual – to having four buckets that need to be kept filled. Each of us will have some energies that resonate more than others and these will already be well topped up. For example, if you are a gym junkie, no doubt your physical energy will get enough refreshing, whereas if you love meditation and connecting with nature, you're keeping your spiritual energy topped up.

Self-awareness and self-belief

We've already discussed the power that self-awareness gives us in helping to make conscious choices and responses. It's just as important to ensure that our self-belief remains intact. This doesn't mean our self-belief has to be unwavering; navigating change can constantly challenge how we relate to ourselves and the decisions we make. It means that we can manage any drop in confidence and recover from challenges and setbacks relatively quickly using a learning mindset. Being aware of our values as leaders means we can make decisions in tune with these values, helping us develop an internal certainty and congruent action.

Connect with others – cultivate mutual support

Leadership is not a solitary act, although often I notice leaders experiencing feelings of isolation, particularly when they become more senior. A strong support network, both inside and outside of work, is fundamental to being able to ask questions, cultivate ideas and brain dump when required.

Make reflection time sacred

The challenge with being a busy leader working in an organisation where action is rewarded, but thinking and reflection are not, is that we're not encouraged to create meaningful habits or routines. Yet every day we are faced with the demands of our roles, challenging communications and triggers which cause reactive emotions, thoughts and actions.

When faced with complex challenges, we need space to unpack and understand our communication and relationships with others so we can make sense of them, explore options and come up with constructive ways forward. Regular and ongoing reflection supports us to understand our experiences and transform the insights we gain into practical strategies for personal growth and organisational impact. It helps us recognise our filters and biases so we can look from a different angle, which opens up possibilities and new ways of thinking, freeing us from the emotional reactions that channel us into fixed and unhelpful thinking. And the more we practise it, the more we are able to move towards reflection in action, noticing ourselves and what is happening around us in a more moment-by-moment way.

Reflection helps us learn to:

- Pay attention to our inner voice or intuition, without necessarily acting on it

- Be present, deal with the here and now

- Notice assumptions, both our own and those being expressed by others

- See patterns, how they play out and their impact

- Shift both what we are seeing and the way we are seeing it

Learning is not an isolated activity. If we open ourselves up to learning, if we allow ourselves the chance to use our everyday experiences to inform us, it happens all the time. Regular reflection allows us to consciously do that.

Schedule reflection time and stick to it. This will ensure you allow yourself the much-needed time to think and deepen your learning. How you do this is up to you; we're all different, and what works for one leader will not work for another. I know of one director who books out the first hour and a half of every week to gather his thoughts on what happened the previous week and consider the week ahead. Another uses her first twenty minutes in the office, a third takes breakfast in a quiet corner of the canteen, while a fourth uses time at the end of the day.

Leaders who really want to be effective book out a decent chunk of time, such as half a day, for planning on a more strategic level. This means they can implement their strategy *and* lead and manage their teams effectively through a strengthened adult ego.

Once reflection time is in your diary, it becomes an immovable event that is vital to your success.

The importance of purpose

One of the challenges of being human is that when we are in our ego survival mode, we get caught up in doing at the expense of thinking. This creates an imbalance so we are vulnerable to our reactive ego traps and behaving in a way that potentially does not help us or others. An approach that can really help us transcend our ego is to get in touch with a higher part of ourselves. We can do this by developing clarity around our purpose.

Purpose can be in both the detail of what we do and the bigger picture. For example, you might ask, 'Why do I need to do my accounts? What purpose does it serve?' This can help you find meaning in completing a task which might not be your favourite, but which you are still responsible for.

Being in touch with our purpose can provide us with a connection to something even more meaningful. This can give us access to inner strength and focus, which can really help us get over ourselves to lead from a much more powerful place.

REALITY CHECK

In which my ego kicks in and my purpose helps me transcend my reaction

I can clearly remember the day I had the conversation with my HR manager when she advised me that my role was at risk. I immediately felt threatened, my ego kicked in and I rebelled, challenging everything she was saying. It was not a great conversation and we were both left feeling shaken and upset.

I took some time out to reflect and consulted with my coach. This helped me understand my reaction and why I had become so defensive. My coach asked what was really important to me and this put me in touch with why I do the work I do. My purpose is to create great places to work, where people can be their best, and to do this by coming from love. I realised that my ego reaction was miles away from what was important to me, so I worked out what would be an approach aligned with my inner purpose.

In my next meeting, I found calm and focus from carrying my purpose with me. The organisation's leaders thought they were being generous by letting me leave immediately, but that did not align with my purpose of creating great places to work. I had a dozen or more internal clients whom I was coaching and it was important to me that their coaching ended well. We therefore negotiated a graduated exit where I would come in to see my clients and conclude their coaching programmes as planned.

At the end of this time period, my HR manager took me to one side and thanked me. She acknowledged how serenely I had managed this period of transition. I appreciated her feedback, but appreciated even more that I'd had a higher purpose that guided me through it.

EGO

Being clear on our overall purpose and reason behind why we do what we do can really help us transcend our ego reactions. Our degree of clarity around our purpose shifts over time, but whatever point we are in our lives, there will be signs of what our purpose is.

Notice for example what brings you the greatest joy and what really angers you. What difference do you tend to make in your work and to the people around you? Where in your life so far have you really given yourself over to a bigger cause beyond yourself? Reflect on these questions and they will give you an indication of what your purpose or emerging purpose is. Then complete this exercise.

EXERCISE

Take some quiet time to do this exercise and make sure you are in a place where you feel calm and won't be disturbed. Play some relaxing music if that helps.

Read each part of this exercise, and then stop, close your eyes and get in touch with whatever you see, hear or feel.

Part 1: Imagine you are much older. You have reached a stage of your life where you feel fulfilled, satisfied; you have achieved all the things you wanted to achieve.

You are invited to attend an awards ceremony, taking place in a large theatre. When you get to the theatre, you notice that the place is full of people you know – loved ones and friends, those you have come into contact with at work. Some you have worked closely with and others less so. You see people from your community. They are all smiling and welcoming you warmly.

Close your eyes and imagine the scene. Who do you see? What are their faces like? What are they saying and how are you feeling?

Part 2: You all take your seats in the theatre. You are sitting with the friends or family you feel closest to.

Someone you admire and respect, a person you have worked with over the years, takes to the stage to start the awards ceremony. They announce that everyone has gathered today to acknowledge one person for their contribution to them individually, to the community and to the world you are a part of. That one person is you. Over the course of the ceremony, several people take to the stage, share the impact you have had and thank you for your contribution.

Close your eyes again, and this time imagine the people who are speaking about you and the sorts of things they are saying.

Part 3: Write down the sorts of things people are saying about your contribution. What difference have you been making to them and the world as a whole? How have you affected them? What are they remembering you for?

When you've written as much as you can, consider what themes are coming through for you. What is important to you in what you want to achieve in your life? Why do you do what you do? What is emerging for you around your life's purpose? How can you start acting from this purpose today?

Summary

Developing our adult ego is an ongoing learning journey, but if we commit to strengthening that part of ourselves, we increase our chances of being able to lead change and take others with us, ensuring a positive outcome. In these demanding times, our personal resilience and resourcefulness are key to ensuring we have the energy to be adult, be conscious when we need to be and act intentionally with the awareness of the impact we can have.

REFLECTION

Consider:

- Where is it easy for you to be adult and where are you vulnerable to child and parent egos being triggered?

- What helps you personally to maintain an adult approach?

- How well do you take care of yourself and your energy levels?

- What action can you take to strengthen your personal foundation even more?

- Where are you guided from your higher purpose and how does this impact you?

8
Building Integrity

We'll explore:

- Redefining integrity
- Why integrity is important when we're navigating egos
- How to restore integrity

Redefining integrity

I ntegrity is one of the fundamental building blocks to both a strong personal foundation and a fully functioning organisation. Yet from my experience of working within organisations, bringing up the subject of integrity can appear to be a trigger, resulting in resistance. People seem to find it difficult to acknowledge that they act with anything but the highest integrity. They feel too vulnerable to admit when they have acted without integrity, which makes it tricky to talk about, let alone rectify.

The *Oxford English Dictionary* definition of integrity is:

> 'The quality of being honest and having strong moral principles… the state of being whole and undivided… the condition of being unified or sound in construction.'[16]

I believe a contributory factor to people's sensitivity to talking about integrity is that the dictionary definition connects it to their moral code, personalising it. Attempts to address a loss of integrity are then perceived as judgemental. In the context of work and making change happen, integrity is much more linked to 'being unified or of sound construction'. Choosing to focus on this interpretation alone takes the personal element out of it and addresses integrity in a simpler way.

Integrity in this context is about whether something is aligned and workable. If a chair has integrity, then it is well constructed and maintained in a condition that will ensure it won't collapse when I sit down. I can rely on it to work. In the human domain, the degree to which we do what we say we will do, both in terms of our promises to others and to ourselves, is what gives us integrity.

Boiling it all down, integrity is about keeping to our word. Do we do as we say we will do? And if we are unable to follow through on what we say we will do, do

---

16   Oxford Dictionary of English [app], OUP/MobiSystems

we take action to let those who will be impacted know? On an organisational level, are people supported to act with integrity? To what degree is there transparency with clear goals, roles and expectations?

This is more than just about being accountable. In the complex and ambiguous terrain of the new normal, maintaining our integrity can be a challenge. As goal posts shift and the need for high performance increases, the chance of our over or under inflated ego kicking in increases, which then risks our integrity slipping. Think about it like spinning plates. The more plates you are spinning, the harder it is to keep all of them going, so there is an increased chance of one of them falling.

When faced with multiple demands, we can find it increasingly hard to be present, meaning we make unconsciously rash decisions that impact our ability to follow through. Opportunities for short cuts tempt us and integrity then slips. Creating a commonly shared understanding of integrity and its impact that removes the moral judgement is the beginning of setting the conditions and conversations where its breakdowns can be addressed and rectified. We are all human; we all make mistakes. It's owning up to and rectifying those mistakes as opposed to covering them up that restores integrity.

This doesn't just apply in the realm of whether we keep our word to others, but also the degree to which we keep our word to ourselves. Being clear of our values and living a life in tune with these provides us with a sense of assuredness and ease which is missing when we act or live in ways that are inconsistent. Being aware of our personal values and what they mean to us gives us a personal framework for living and leading. When we act in alignment with these, then our integrity is consistent; we are keeping our word to ourselves. This is fundamental to being a leader. It helps us create congruence between our decisions, actions and words at the most minute level.

Think about people you have come across – some will be in your workplace – who for whatever reason don't inspire trust in you. There is something that just doesn't add up. Maybe it's a lack of sincerity, or they're slightly overbearing, but how they present while appearing well intentioned doesn't quite connect. Perhaps they're smiling too broadly when delivering bad news, or promising but not delivering. This is inauthenticity and a sign that ego and potential games are at play. The impact is a loss of trust, risking levels of engagement and performance. What causes this slight but impactful disconnection is an incongruence between their word, be it to themselves, and living in tune with their values, or to others.

Why integrity is important when navigating egos

The bottom line of integrity is all about delivering what we say we will deliver, fulfilling our promises to ourselves and to others. When we do this it creates a sense of power and strength within ourselves. If we respond with integrity to others, this leads to the establishment of trust.

When we lack integrity, the greatest impact is a loss of power and energy, which results in us being more liable to be triggered, less present, more vulnerable to getting into unhelpful games and the focus of our attention being out of kilter with our intentions. For example, when in a game, we unconsciously act out a role which is dysfunctional. This means we are likely to misinterpret reality. Our controlling parent or adapted child will muddy our reactions and responses. This leads to communication breakdowns and avoidance of real, authentic conversations, which are necessary to creating an engaged, high-performing organisational culture.

How to restore integrity

On a personal level

Look around you and notice where you are not living life in tune with your values. Where are you acting out of a need to please others and/or prove yourself at the cost of being who you really are?

EXERCISE

Make a list of all the things you are tolerating, not just in work, but in the whole of your life. This could be the smallest thing such as a button that needs tightening on a jacket to a relationship where you are holding something back. Write as many things as you can think of. The more, the better.

Over the next month, take action to address each thing. Start with the easiest one first. Notice over the course of the month the impact of addressing your tolerations has on your energy levels.

On a relationship level

Integrity impacts our relationships on many levels, from whether we obviously fulfil our promises to the degree we say what we truly feel. The reality of our busy lives is that there are times we promise to deliver on something, but circumstances arise that mean we don't fulfil our promise. When these circumstances arise, we can do something about it by getting in touch with the people we know it will impact and rearranging. But there are times when we don't fulfil on our promise and let another person or other people down.

There are various ways to respond:

• Ignore what happened and hope the affected party/ies didn't notice

- Take action to cover up the mistake – for example, destroying all evidence or making up an excuse

- Own up to our responsibility and make amends

While it may seem that the third option is the most obvious one, I have seen the first two happen many times within an organisation. For example, I've seen a senior leader destroying all evidence of his team's negative feedback to avoid being taken to task by his line manager, and a whole division changing the terms of their agreements to achieve budget, with massive impact on their relationships with suppliers and stress placed on the level of leadership held responsible for making it happen.

Although the third option is the obvious choice, it takes something for us to follow that option. It takes a preparedness to be vulnerable; a preparedness to own up to the fact that we got it wrong; the ability to let go of making excuses for ourselves and getting over whatever shame or embarrassment we may feel. It is likely in the scenario where we are the cause of the broken agreement that our internal controlling parent will be adopting a highly critical tone, while our internal adapted child will want to crawl into a corner or make all sorts of excuses to cover up or blame others. This is when our self-awareness and self-management are invaluable. Only by catching ourselves in those moments do we create a choice around how we respond to them, thus avoiding a defensive and ultimately unhelpful reaction.

REALITY CHECK

In which I let a client down and have to deal with myself to stay in integrity

I recently missed an important client call. This call had been really difficult to set up as my client was so busy, so I was pleased when we could find what seemed like the only slot to make it work.

On the day of our call, I was immersed in writing a rather demanding and complicated proposal which preoccupied me for the majority of the day. I'd noted that morning that my client call was in the evening and looked forward to speaking with them later, but as the day progressed, my head became full of the proposal I was writing and I inadvertently missed the call. By the time I realised this, it was too late to catch any time with my client.

My initial reaction was one of shock and horror at the realisation that I was fully responsible. My inner critical parent had a field day, resulting in me feeling really bad for making the mistake. Moving on to feeling ashamed and embarrassed, I then found myself thinking of various reasons I could give for my mistake so that I wouldn't look so bad in my client's eyes, but when I sat back with my hand on my heart, there wasn't one that would be completely honest. And even if there had been, it wouldn't have interested my client. The issue for them was the missed call, not the reason it didn't happen.

I emailed my client, choosing my wording carefully; I wanted to make sure I came from a place where we were both OK. I apologised, shared my embarrassment,

> didn't give an excuse, owned my responsibility for the breakdown, expressed concern for the inconvenience and made a suggestion for what we could do going forward. My client's response was one of understanding and we rescheduled.

By fully embracing and taking responsibility, I allowed the integrity in our relationship to be restored. In this instance, my client was understanding, but equally they would have had the right to be frustrated and annoyed. I might have felt uncomfortable with that, but in the spirit of being responsible, I would have accepted it and understood.

When we're restoring integrity after a breakdown, it is important to take personal responsibility, open up the communication channels and keep them open so the relationship can rebuild and keep moving forward.

Summary

Integrity when it comes to leadership and managing our own and other people's egos is largely linked to keeping our word to ourselves and to others. When we follow through on agreements and are open and honest to ourselves and others, living life in tune with our values, we sleep more easily and maintain our personal power. This makes navigating relationships and change easier as we are able to focus our energy and be more present to each situation we face.

It takes a degree of getting over ourselves to own up and restore our integrity when we need to, but the more we do this, the greater our capacity will be to build trust and lead authentically.

REFLECTION

- Where is it easy for you to keep to your word?

- Where is it more challenging?

- Where might you be compromising your own values?

- What are you tolerating that isn't working for you?

Consider one of the above in greater depth and reflect on what it is that is really holding you back here. What action are you willing to take to address this?

9
Conscious Conversations That Matter

We'll explore:

- Contracting conversations
- The different levels a contracting conversation addresses
- The three Cs of contracting

Over my many years of being a leadership consultant and coach, I have noticed that leading change effectively depends on the quality of relationships throughout the organisation. This is influenced by the ability of leaders to have good, open, and honest conversations. If we want people to be engaged, then the process is a two-way conversation. It's important to make time to allow such conversations to happen so people can ask questions, share concerns, gain clarity, set expectations and move forward. If change isn't happening, it's time to look at the type and nature of conversations that are going on.

Contracting conversations

There are certain conscious conversations that enable us to build and sustain strong, effective, collaborative relationships with others, giving us a chance to transcend our egos and create a cornerstone for navigating change. Like many important conversations, how we conduct ourselves and a degree of preparation and thoughtfulness in our approach will make a difference. This is not so we can prepare a script and make sure we have the right words, but to guage how we are reacting. We can then increase our awareness of what we want from the conversation and focus on how we need to be during it.

For example, being upset with one of my team members and judging them, will impact my ability to address them in a reasonable adult way. I need to be conscious of my judgement and manage myself to talk to my team member in a manner that supports a constructive way forward that they are engaged with.

A really important conversation to have, both at the beginning and throughout our working relationships, is a contracting conversation. If you have ever been coached, you may well have experienced a contracting conversation where the coach discussed with you how you want to work together. This will include raising and addressing assumptions you and the coach may have about the context for coaching, the relationship and each other's responsibilities. The intention of this conversation is to create a foundation of psychological safety, where the coachee feels free to be themselves and do their best thinking, and the coach is free to challenge and support their coachee's needs as appropriate.

Where there are two or more people in the workplace who rely on each other for support and/or delivery of a result, this type of conversation is absolutely valid.

Think about how relationships work. Let's start by considering how we create relationships on a one-to-one basis.

In the context of work, we meet the people in our network, be it our team reports, manager, peers or other stakeholders, and the conversation is all about the job there is to do. Generally, we pay little attention to how we need to be in the doing of that job, so we have one-dimensional conversations about something that is multi-dimensional.

The term 'contract' may make you think of something legal and binding. Although this type of conversation doesn't involve lawyers, it does create clarity and agreement on how the relationship will be conducted and helps both parties understand each other's needs and expectations, and more importantly, feel safe.

Contracting can help create effective relationships through using an adult-to-adult conversation where both parties have the opportunity to contribute their thoughts, feelings, needs and expectations of each other to make the implicit explicit. The benefits include surfacing otherwise unspoken assumptions and expectations, and creating a safe and secure basis from which to conduct a relationship. The latter is particularly important for establishing trust and the space for people to engage and bring themselves and their full potential to work.

The different levels a contracting conversation addresses

Contracting in relation to work takes place at different levels:

1. Administrative – the logistics and processes, eg work from home or office

2. Role specific – objectives, roles and responsibilities of each party

3. Psychological – unspoken beliefs and expectations of each party over and above those in the first two points, eg a team member expecting to be noticed for their efforts, or a divisional director expecting their team to be flexible

Administrative

When we take a job, we sign a legal contract which spells out the organisation's expectations of us and what we will receive from the organisation in return. It is all about the logistics and practicalities that support the working relationship.

Role specific

The intended result is for both parties in the relationship to be clear of what is required and agree how they will work together. Professional contracting addresses these expectations and needs and creates agreement for how they will be met. For example, a manager expects they will be kept updated on a monthly basis on the progress of the project they've delegated to their team member, while the team member needs to know that they can go to their manager whenever they need support in relation to the project.

Making something like this explicit is an important part of effective working relationships. It not only establishes clarity for both parties, but also creates agreement. If those agreements are at risk of getting broken, the fact it is an agreement makes it easier to address. When something is stated clearly in the first place, if it doesn't happen, it becomes a piece of factual data to discuss on an adult-to-adult basis, rather than an emotive issue that could risk reactive adapted child or controlling parent responses.

If the manager in the previous example finds their team member is cancelling monthly meetings and not seeking any support, then they can refer to the fact this was an explicit agreement around how they would work together. This makes it easier to raise and enquire into the subject than if no agreement had been put in place.

We can create even greater clarity by following up any contracting conversation in writing, specifying our understanding of what has been agreed.

Psychological

The psychological element of a contract is often the most challenging to make explicit because it involves the underlying and often unconscious beliefs and assumptions we hold about ourselves and the other person. For the most part, when a relationship is working and there is a good alliance, we may not need to delve into the psychological contract, but if there are unmet needs, confusion, differences that we don't understand, it is helpful to explore our assumptions and beliefs, along with those of the other party, and how they impact the way we work together.

REALITY CHECK

In which Luke needs to find a way to work with his line manager

Luke was a director I worked with who was struggling with the attitude of his line manager. No matter how well he did, his manager never gave him any positive feedback and seemed only to criticise and push harder.

Luke eventually sat down with his manager and shared how he experienced their style. The line manager's response was revealing. It turned out they believed that when working at a director level, people shouldn't need positive reinforcement and that all criticism contributed to an individual's growth and development.

Surfacing his line manager's guiding beliefs opened Luke's eyes to understanding why they behaved as they did. He didn't necessarily like his manager's approach, but having had the conversation, he could manage his own needs in a different way and be less reliant on his manager for this.

The three Cs of contracting

A contracting conversation is not a one-off. The contract will change as the relationship develops and the demands of the organisation shift, so it is an organic way to check, develop and understand the relationship, with the contract being amended through re-contracting conversations. A contracting conversation can also take place at specific events and with groups of people. They are useful conversations whenever there is a need to create clarity around expectations and agreements and are a basic foundation in creating psychological safety.

There are different types of contracting conversation. I refer to these as the three Cs of contracting, which relate to creating contracts within a certain space and time.

C1 - takes place at the beginning of a relationship, such as a leader working with a new team member. It can also be useful for reviewing how a relationship is working. This conversation puts in place basic understandings and agreements for how each party would like the relationship to work overall. The goal is to make expectations explicit and clear. This conversation can be returned to as often as either party deems necessary to keep the relationship working at an optimum.

C2 - takes place at the beginning of an event, such as a meeting or 1:1, to check what each party wants from the discussion.

C3 - takes place in the moment, for example noticing someone's behaviour and agreeing with them to give feedback.

Contracting is influenced by the circumstances within which you are engaging with the other person. Is the relationship one that requires you to deliver certain results? If so, what are they? How much certainty surrounds the relationship? How well do you know each other? What do each of you need from the relationship?

Let's have a look at each C in more detail.

C1 Contracting

This is an exploratory conversation to ascertain each party's needs and wants in terms of making expectations clear and creating an overall effective working relationship. Areas and questions to be addressed could include:

- What is each party's understanding of the purpose of this relationship?

- What does each party want or need from this working relationship?

- What expectations do they need to make explicit?

- What could get in the way of this relationship being effective?

- What can they do to prevent this or address this should it arise?

- How do people like to be managed or led?

- How would each party describe their communication style?

- How do they like to receive feedback?

- What assumptions does each person hold about the other parties and about their relationship?

- What in the bigger organisational system could impact this relationship, either positively or negatively?

- How does each party want to respond to this?

- What specific agreements do they want to put in place to support this relationship?

- How and when will they review how the relationship is working?

C2 Contracting

This is a signposting conversation to establish success criteria and support focus for a particular event, for example a performance review meeting.

- What does each party want/need from this?

- How will they know they've got what they wanted?

- How can everyone best work together today?

C3 Contracting

This is an in-the-moment agreement. It could include asking permission to give feedback, noticing something that is impacting progress, getting agreement to move the process on, or picking up on an atmosphere and making it explicit to help inform everyone.

Questions to ask or points to raise could include:

- Can I offer you some feedback?

- I notice that... For example, I notice that we keep laughing about this when it's serious. We seem to be avoiding sorting this out.

- We've spent some time discussing this. Is it time now to draw a conclusion and move on?

- What can we do to lighten the mood here?

Conducting contracting conversations with the people you work with closely provides a foundation to creating effective relationships. It is a pre-emptive step to supporting healthy, constructive communication, where both parties feel OK and triggering of reactive egos is kept to a minimum. Agreements made explicit in a contract provide boundaries, which in turn create a sense of safety and the building of trust.

While contracting conversations will support helpful communication, they don't mean that things will not go awry sometimes. But having a contract helps pinpoint the means to address this and provides a frame of reference for conversations which might otherwise be more difficult.

Summary

A contracting conversation is a valuable tool for pro-actively setting out needs, expectations, beliefs and assumptions and managing potential ego traps. This helps make needs and wants from a relationship explicit as opposed to implicit and provides a foundation of psychological safety. It is an adult-to-adult conversation that puts a relationship on a firm footing of awareness and integrity for both parties and makes it easier to address misunderstandings and differences when they arise.

REFLECTION

Think about different relationships that are important to you at work. Select one or two and consider:

- How clear are you of the other person's expectations and needs from you?

- What assumptions are going on between you?

Then think about what you would like to do to strengthen the contract and relationship you have with them.

10
How A Coaching Approach Can Help

We'll explore:

- Growing with your role

- Using coaching to enable others

- What coaching is and isn't

- One helpful mindset and two valuable skills

- A strategic approach to self

Growing with your role

Coaching in the context of leading others is all about peeling back the layers of self-awareness to notice behaviour and change habits. For example, let's say I have a long-term habit of pleasing others. This habit has many advantages as it means I am reliable, supportive, a good listener and ensure those around me are happy. All admirable qualities and strengths. But as I navigate through the organisation and my career has traction, the demands placed on me change. I need to stick my neck out, break away from always pleasing others and risk being disliked. All rich in triggering ego-centred reactions.

Coaching can help me get clear on what is going on and how I might take on new ways of being. I will always have the underlying drive to please, but rather than being monopolised by it, I can learn with the help of coaching to transcend it and develop a selection of ways to be so I am in a position of awareness and choice.

Coaching can certainly help you grow in your role and become familiar with your internal processes and ego. It can also be a powerful tool for supporting others. As a skillset for you as a leader, coaching is invaluable in getting the most out of others at all levels.

Using coaching to enable others

Coaching offers so much to both leaders and the people they lead. Over the last thirty years, it has emerged as one of the most potent leadership tools for enabling high performance and engagement. The leader who takes a coaching approach both supports and challenges them-selves and the people they lead to go beyond what they see as possible, strengthen capability, develop intelligent insights and practise ways of being that enhance results.

It is an intentional approach that utilises the positive elements of ego. The nature we adopt when coaching someone else is based on getting over ourselves and being there for the other.

Coaching can often be misinterpreted and misunderstood by organisations and their leaders, so let's put some clarity around what coaching is and isn't and what attitudes and beliefs support effective coaching.

What coaching is and isn't

	Coaching is:	Coaching is not:
Overall	A conversation focused on supporting another to access their own resources and solutions	Telling or suggesting to someone what to do, fixing the problem for them
Ego states	Adult, supported by some free child and little professor, and nurturing parent	Controlling parent, adapted child
Attitude	Open and curious Trusting the process Balancing challenge and support Respecting the coachee as an adult	Attached to being the expert Anxious to take action Overly challenging or supportive Infantilising the coachee

	Coaching is:	Coaching is not:
Beliefs	I'm OK, you're OK	I'm OK, you're not OK
	Win-win	I'm right, you're wrong
	Believing every person has the resources they need to make a choice	Believing I must pass on the answer because I've been there before
	Ensuring every person strives to learn, grow and become best version of themselves	There isn't time for the coachee to find their own solution
Skills	Being present	Listening while really waiting to speak
	Quietening your judgemental inner voice	Closed questions
	Open questions	

Misinterpretation of coaching and the need to get things done quickly results in leaders often having trouble leaving well-worn habits behind and struggling to develop the attitude and skills that enable powerful coaching. Employed for our experience and the things that we know, we can find it hard to let go of always needing to have the answer. Never is that more true than when we're endeavouring to coach someone, particularly if we already have first-hand experience of what that person may be going through and think we know the answer. Coaching is riddled with opportunities for our ego to take over and diminish the chance for someone to do their own thinking and make a breakthrough in their development.

Being under constant pressure to achieve results contributes to us as leaders being vulnerable to moving into automatic pilot mode, leaving the way wide open for our ego to be activated. This results in us often finding it hard to let go of the need to advise and fix, falling into the trap of telling team members what to do, either directly or more subtly through the use of leading questions. Whenever we are advising or leading, we are not coaching, because coaching in its purest form requires us to let go of our own ego and come from a place of not knowing and being curious. Yet coaching is when getting over our own ego can be hardest to do.

Imagine someone from your team comes to you with a challenge they are facing. You have dealt with it many times before, so it is the easiest thing in the world for you to tell them what to do. To instruct or advise is an approach you can choose to take, and for some situations it will be the most appropriate one and will have an impact. Whenever you tell or advise someone to do something, you are not empowering them. In fact, rather than enabling them to develop confidence in their own thinking and initiative, you create a dependency that risks them returning to you time and time again.

This is a common game that leaders and team members find themselves in. The team member develops learned helplessness (in other words, they become a victim) and the leader becomes the rescuer. While this may work as a short-term strategy, it has consequences in that it risks the potential for growth. Then the leader gets bogged down in dealing with the operational details that their team could be addressing, rather than being freed up to work on strategic priorities.

As a leader coaching your team, don't fall into the trap of telling people what to do. You are not empowering them to deal with their own problems and risk having those problems passed to you. This is brilliantly illustrated by Kenneth Blanchard in his book *The One Minute Manager Meets The Monkey*.[17] Blanchard uses the metaphor of a monkey to describe a problem. He talks about managers and team members having their own set of monkeys.

What typically happens is that a team member will go to their manager with their monkey (problem) and the manager will say, 'No worries, give that to me and I'll sort it out for you.' The manager is then swamped with monkeys, while the team member has none.

REALITY CHECK

In which a leader is overwhelmed with monkeys

When I first worked with Aisha, a director in a large blue-chip manufacturer, she was stressed, overwhelmed and close to exhaustion. My first

17   Blanchard, K, Burrows, H and Oncken, W (1990) *The One Minute Manager Meets The Monkey: Free up your time and deal with priorities*. London: Thorsons

session with her took place late afternoon in her office, which was surrounded by her department's open-plan working space. Aisha talked about the long hours she worked, in at seven in the morning and often not leaving until gone eight in the evening.

By now it was after 5pm and I noticed that all of Aisha's team had left. I asked about this and Aisha admitted that she was unique in her long hours. She'd never known her team to ever work late, but she had so many things to do she felt compelled to stay.

Her support of her team was unwavering, but she was tolerating at least one person underperforming and didn't like to put upon the capable team members who were ready to develop. This opened up a whole new conversation about Aisha's confidence as a leader and her tendency to avoid making demands of people. Rather than coaching them, she let them pass all their monkeys on to her.

Our work together focused on helping her strengthen her adult ego state, set clearer boundaries with people, delegate and coach her team, thus increasing their capability and enabling her to take greater control over her own workload and improve her life balance and wellbeing.

As Aisha's situation illustrates, to help ourselves and others, we need to let go of our ego attachment to being the person with all the answers and focus on the potential of the person in front of us to access their own resources and develop their capability. Leading a team through change and charting unknown waters requires people who can think for themselves and work things out. A leader who has taken the time to coach their people by being present, asking open questions and keeping to each coachee's agenda will be supporting them to do this and developing their leadership potential at the same time.

Coaching essentially teaches people to learn. To help you as a leader, it enables leadership from others. It raises self-awareness, understanding and supports you and your team to be more effective through taking meaningful action.

EXERCISE

Sit back and reflect on your approach when coaching others. Look at each question and note how you rate your performance on a scale of 1 to 10 (1 being not at all and 10 being all the time) when coaching a member of your team.

How much are you able to:

- Let go of your own agenda?

- Be present and quieten your judgemental inner voice?

- Ask open questions?

- Help your team member explore their thinking?

- Help your team member come up with their own ideas for action?

One helpful mindset and two valuable skills

As a leader who is coaching, you need to be self-aware and conscious of your own ego and the traps you may fall into. Attending a coaching skills programme will help you develop many more approaches than I can mention here, but from working with leaders to help them develop a coaching approach, I have found there are three main things that repeatedly come through. These three things make the biggest difference to not only supporting team members grow, but also helping the leader understand their team members so much better, strengthening their relationship and commitment to each other's success. One is a mindset, the other two are valuable skills.

The first is developing a mindset of curiosity. It's much harder to jump into fixing and giving all the answers if we are genuinely curious and open to understanding someone else's perspective. Being curious is also a great antidote to being judgemental. When we find ourselves judging (which is a perfectly human thing to do), it's a sign that our ego is definitely active, whereas if we shift away from judging towards being curious, it supports an open and learning approach.

REALITY CHECK

In which a leader creates huge success through being curious

Joanna was a much sought-after MD with the reputation for building highly effective teams and turning around company performance. People who worked with her, from her team to her clients and suppliers, always spoke highly of her.

What set Joanna apart was her infectious personality and ability to connect with people and put them at ease. One of the things she regarded as a key strength was that she was nosey, but not in an invasive way. Joanna was genuinely interested and curious about people, their concerns and their views of the world. This meant she was not afraid to ask questions others might avoid or share her observations non-judgementally of what she saw going on. Her curiosity also meant she let go of preconceived ideas, instead exploring possibilities which encouraged innovation and generated the success of the businesses she led.

EXERCISE

Next time you find yourself being triggered and having an extreme reaction to something, shift your mindset to one of being curious. Ask yourself some open questions and wonder about why you have reacted like this. It's interesting to see how your mood can shift by just getting interested in your own process rather than allowing your emotions to dominate you.

On another occasion, practise observing a situation, perhaps a discussion in a meeting, and just be curious about what is being said and how people are being. Notice the difference in your own response when you're taking this mindset as opposed to how you might normally respond.

Coaching is a relational approach that lends itself to co-creative, conversational leadership. This makes it highly engaging and empowering, which is where it can have such a great impact. A coaching conversation is a two-way interaction which meets people's needs to be included, feel powerful and acknowledged. The time given to coaching fulfils these needs through the two most valuable skills of listening and asking open questions.

The quality of listening you give to another through coaching communicates whether or not you consider that they matter. The challenge and support you offer through open questioning empowers the coachee to access their own resources and solutions, and the very nature of coaching as a person-centred activity means the whole process is an acknowledging one. But there are different ways to listen which are affected by how much you are being driven by your own ego needs as opposed to consciously engaging and coming from a place of openness and curiosity.

Level 1: Listening while waiting to speak

We may appear to be listening. We may be giving our attention to the other person and even be demonstrating non-verbal signals of listening, but inside our head, we are actually paying attention to our own inner dialogue, making decisions and judgements about what the other person is saying, or trying to think of and remember a really good question to ask. When we listen at this level, our listening is superficial.

Level 2: Listening with laser-like attention

When listening at this level, we keep our attention focused on the other person, concentrating on what they are saying and listening to the words and way they say them to understand how they may be feeling. We may even paraphrase and summarise what we have heard.

Level 3: Listening while being fully present

Being fully present means being in the moment with the other person, listening with deep connection. This creates the space to let go of any past experiences or judgements and come from a place of possibility, enabling access to alternative views and insights that the other levels of listening could limit. Our judgement disappears as we appreciate fully where the other person is coming from.

Level three takes much more intention and practice than the other two levels. Even experienced coaches may move around all three levels during a coaching conversation; the key is to be conscious of how we are listening and the way our judgements can impact this. Noticing when we slip into judgements gives us a chance to do something about it and focus on listening from a deeper level.

EXERCISE

Think about a time when someone really listened to you from a place of complete openness.

- What was that experience like for you?

- How did the quality of their listening impact you?

Think of another time when you listened to someone from level two or three.

- What impact did your quality of listening have on the conversation?

- What enabled you to listen in that way?

The other side of listening, and part of being curious, is the ability to ask good questions. And the type of questions that are really going to help the other person gain insight and learn are the ones which encourage their thinking to be stretched so they can explore alternative views.

The questions that help are open questions. When you're listening from levels two and three, questions often form naturally from what your coachee is saying. As a leader, you can then let go of worrying about getting the question wrong. In fact, in the coaching world, if you focus on keeping your questions open, it's almost impossible to ask a question that is unhelpful. Open questions can be challenging as that helps your team member to think through their motives and preconceived thinking, and reach beyond where they have thought before.

Focus on using questions that ask what and how. Use the why question to explore someone's motives and values, but be particularly mindful of using this question in an open and curious way. The why question, coming from a controlling parent ego state, can be perceived as punitive and blaming and can have the opposite effect you may have intended.

A strategic approach to self

In an earlier chapter, we discussed that the dynamics of the conversation we are participating in can shift in a split second, so we can be more effective if we slow down. Coaching as an approach does take time, because its power is in slowing down to ultimately speed up.

When involved in a coaching conversation, we are effectively stepping back from the action to reflect and take a different viewpoint so that we can break patterns of behaviour and activities that are not working. This is essentially a strategic thinking activity, which so many leaders struggle with as they step up from operational manager to enterprise leader. Leading at a more strategic level requires us to manage our egos to even greater effect, and developing our ability to coach is a great tool to support us with this. Being able to coach others requires us to maintain an openness to our own learning and development, which in itself means that we will be role modelling a way of being that transcends more ego-driven needs to look to the bigger picture and greater cause.

Summary

Coaching offers us a great opportunity to navigate our own and others' egos because it requires an adult-to-adult conversation. Our mindset, quality of listening and use of open questions all enable us to transcend our ego-driven desire to fix and advise, utilising our integrated adult instead.

A coaching approach provides not only the opportunity to empower and support our teams to grow, but also a framework and way of being that continually supports us to manage ourselves, keep building self-awareness and be present. This puts us in a stronger position to manage the relationships and egos going on around us.

REFLECTION

- How do you use coaching to support you or people around you?

- What coaching skills or mindset are you particularly good at?

- Which do you wish to practise more of?

11
Navigating Ego To
Enable Culture Change

We'll explore:

- How ego affects an organisation's culture

- The trickiness of shifting culture

- The games that go on

- Making culture change happen

- Ongoing development over a period of time

How ego affects an organisation's culture

Above all else, an organisation is a large collection of people who have come together to cause something to happen, be it making widgets, providing service excellence, making money, doing good, spending responsibly or a whole selection of these and other things. The culture of an organisation sets the tone for how the collective group of people act, and the way leaders behave directly influences an organisation's culture. Leaders' behaviour amplifies the way work gets done on a day-to-day basis, embedding organisational practices that reflect shared beliefs, values and assumptions. This has a massive impact on the way the organisation does business and treats its people, customers, suppliers and shareholders.

Considering the nature of an organisation as a collection of people, and that each individual person has their own ego, we could say that an organisation's culture is actually the collective ego of all the people working there. For example, I was recently coaching a leader who had gained employment with a new organisation and was excitedly talking about moving from one organisation to another. She was conscious of the different cultures of each organisation, and when she described each one, it was as if she were describing a person. The words she used were character traits, saying both organisations were caring, people focused, committed to service excellence and making a positive difference, while one occurred to her as being more open and transparent than the other.

The role of leaders and leadership behaviour shapes the organisation's culture through the leadership shadow it creates. How a leader's mood, attitude and action influence the climate and culture around them creates what are called cultural norms, often represented by the popular phrase 'It's how we do things around here'.

Such norms can give an organisation its character, picked up in the language that is acceptable, the rituals and routines, environment, overt or covert politics and power, and the way people are treated. These become embedded and are often invisible to those working there.

Some examples of norms I've observed from different organisations are:

- **Ritual** – monthly special breakfasts to welcome new starters

- **Language** – when describing how to get on in a particular organisation, people repeated the phrase 'You need big elbows to push yourself in'

- **Environment** – immaculate and orderly, every chair in the boardroom left in exactly the right place

- **Power politics** – room space in a department is currency for power and influence

- **People** – you need a constant senior sponsor to get ahead, and moving overseas risks the loss of visibility and sponsorship

- **Processes** – anxiety around ensuring safety results in 50,000 documented step-by-step processes

EXERCISE

Consider different organisations you have contact with. It could be any organisation, for example the tax office or a hotel. What is:

- The demeanour of the staff you have contact with?

- The process you are asked to participate in?

- The overall effect your contact with this organisation has on you?

Ask yourself, if this organisation were a person, what sort of person would they be?

- What impression do you gain of the culture this organisation has?

- What beliefs and values do you think are important to it?

- What would you imagine the leaders of this organisation to be like?

Now do this process again, but this time imagine you are a Martian, visiting earth for the first time. You are looking at the organisation you work for through completely neutral eyes. What insights are emerging for you?

Trickiness of shifting culture

Enabling a positive cultural change is often enigmatic and challenging because, much like our ego reactions, culture lies largely in the area of the unconscious. This blindness makes it hard to put our fingers on precisely what it is, and if we aren't aware of it, then it's nigh on impossible to do anything about it.

REALITY CHECK

Where my own behaviour is impacted by cultural norms

I once worked internally as a coach for a large corporation. I began my role full of enthusiasm for what I could contribute to the senior board I was a part of. In my early weeks, I could see behaviours and attitudes that were helpful and unhelpful to the team's effectiveness, but as my time progressed, it became increasingly hard not to be consumed by the team's cultural norms. I developed the same cultural blindness as my colleagues, resulting in my finding it incredibly difficult to impact any change.

In hindsight, I can see that my own ego was activated, resulting in my losing confidence and playing it safe. I concentrated on building relationships with individuals and lost focus on the team as an entity. This mirrored how each team member behaved; it was as if my vision became blurred and I could no longer see the behaviours it was part of my job to call out.

Culture is created through habitual behaviours and ways of being that are out of reach of our levels of awareness. Trying to shift culture is hard because we cannot grasp it; we get sucked back into it without our knowledge. It is like a fish swimming in water with no concept of what water is. Take the fish out of water, it gasps for breath and gets what water is; put it back in, water becomes the norm again.

This is why people leave stand-alone training initiatives and team events inspired with capabilities and commitments to new ways of working, yet sometimes within days have resorted to previous behaviours, despite good intentions to the contrary. For a day or two, leaders are removed from the work stream and are able to see the culture and way of being for what it is. Then when they return to the stream, the culture is like a current that pulls them back into old ways of being and maintaining the cultural status quo, often without them being aware of it. I like to describe this as the 'cultural drift', because it's a bit like when we swim in the river or sea. We often cannot see the current, but we unknowingly get caught up in it, and before we know it, we are drifting with it. It then takes energy to swim against it.

It's not only the blindness to cultural drift, but also the collection of many people that makes it tricky to change. Just as each individual leader has a blind spot to their behaviour and how it impacts others, so does the organisation to its culture, and it's even harder to shift it due to the complex nature of it being a collective ego.

The games that go on

I've often come across the term 'smoke and mirrors' in the context of what is going on, particularly at the more senior levels of an organisation. When I hear this term, it's a warning bell to the fact that games are happening with egos being activated on many levels. This then has an impact on the integrity of the whole organisation.

REALITY CHECK

In which HR meets resistance

Pam the HR director was keen to engage Frank in tackling performance more directly and wanted to introduce a new performance management scheme. In the executive meeting, she was met with hostility and rejection by Frank, who felt that it was not his or his manager's responsibility to be doing the job of HR.

The attack by Frank on Pam's scheme was actually a cover-up for what was really going on. Frank was not the most popular of leaders and had some unhappy people on his team. The new scheme would support people to share their experiences of their managers and leaders, and it was an easier option to criticise and blame HR than engage with addressing his own and his department's issues.

This is an example of a team dynamic, but the challenge of cultural norms and smoke-and-mirrors game playing is that it can become a company-wide phenomenon.

This can ultimately have a catastrophic impact on the whole organisation's performance.

REALITY CHECK

In which collective unconscious behaviours and mindset lead to real financial trouble

People within a certain organisation prided themselves on the fact that, year on year, they achieved target. Leaders were promoted to senior levels, including the main board, based on achieving this deliverable. The implicit and unspoken cultural message was 'We have to hit target at any cost'. This was particularly important to keep shareholders happy.

In one particular division, it was really clear three months before the deadline that the target was not going to be met. Directors delegated the task of resolving this to their heads of departments. To address the shortfall, the solution was for all departments to review spending and push payment of any outstanding invoices into the following financial year. There was a frenzy of update meetings to make this happen.

From speaking to senior managers, I discovered that this was a regular event to ensure targets were achieved. I observed the collective group's behaviour with concern. My perspective was that surely one day, the chickens would come home to roost and the organisation wouldn't be able to do this anymore as there would be a massive shortfall.

In one meeting, I was curious and asked the question, 'What's going to happen when you can't push the payments forward anymore?' This was met by an incredulous response.

'This is called creative accountancy, it's how we do it every year.'

This was a large organisation that wielded a lot of power in its marketplace. The unspoken part of the senior managers' response was the implication that 'A company of our size and standing can get away with this'. Or maybe the collective thinking and belief was so strong that they didn't even consider this practice as risky.

Some years later, the creative accountancy came to light and caused serious problems for the organisation's financial results and reputation. The collective and unconscious view that the company was infallible certainly fed into the trouble it eventually found itself in.

What feeds into tricky team and organisational dynamics is a lack of explicitness about expectations and needs across the senior team, which then trickles down into the organisation. This often leads to an agenda and way of being that is built on assumptions, lack of clarity and safety.

Lack of safety provides a breeding ground for conscious or unconscious ego-centred anxiety that triggers defensive ego behaviour. In the reality check, 'hit target at all costs' was the collective message and there was a strong parent-to-child dynamic. This caused the managers who were delegated with the task to comply with their directors' demands. The blindness to the dynamics and underlying fear made it almost impossible for people to speak out and push back against their senior leaders, and even if they did, the norm of the situation meant their feedback was met with denial and rejection. It was not OK to challenge, so lack of safety and security fed into people complying with behaviours and actions that, if they'd had the chance to step back and look at from a distance, they would probably have recognised as not being workable.

How can we be alert to some of the signs and symptoms of the unhelpful and potentially destructive ego games going on at an organisational level? Take a look at how your organisation's most senior team is behaving. There are some common and specific behaviours at senior level that are strong indicators and impact the wider organisation. These include:

- Little if any trust, illustrated through talking behind others' backs, lack of personal sharing and vulnerability

- Scapegoating – where one particular division is the brunt of all criticism

- Splitting – division and polarity into two distinct viewpoints, each making the other wrong

- Pairing – two members align and talk as one voice

- False compliance – nodding heads to team leader direction in the meeting, not following directions outside

- Lack of challenge, debate and constructive conflict

- Communication that appears to go around in circles, eg the same things being discussed from one meeting to the next

- Siloing – leaders being protective of their own specific domain, putting this first rather than the higher strategic view of the executive team

- When being held to account, pushing responsibility elsewhere

- All of these behaviours seemingly being beyond the control of the leader of the team

This is quite a list, but I've placed it here to help identify behaviours that have a negative impact on the effectiveness of not just the team they are present on, but also the most senior executive teams. The knock-on effect to organisational performance will be dramatic.

Making culture change happen

When we're creating a culture of increased high performance and engagement, the terrain is complex. Complexity requires a variety of approaches, each interdependent on and supportive of the other. Using a variety of approaches increases the ability to deal with the cultural drift, just as a team of rowers in a large boat will have more chance of tackling a strong current than a single canoeist.

Here are some key lessons I've learned from various culture-change projects, highlighting the different elements that I have found to work.

Start at the top – responsible senior leadership

When we bear in mind the influence that leaders' behaviour has on the culture of an organisation, there is little doubt that those in leadership roles, right from the top, have a need to step up and be responsible for the impact of their behaviour and attitude. I have yet to see any change happen, or even achieve momentum, when senior-level sponsorship is missing. And sponsorship is more than the senior leader nodding their head to the culture change; it requires leaders to actively and relentlessly champion change, really living the behaviours of the new culture and supporting their colleagues and teams to do the same. This takes persistence, determination and a dogged belief in the value of the change. Role modelling is the greatest form of influence – just look at children copying their parents – so there is a need for leaders to increase their mindfulness around how they act and the message their behaviour is sending out to others.

As a young consultant, I was commissioned to run assertiveness courses for middle managers and team leaders. The challenge that I consistently heard from participants was that it was all well and good them learning these skills, but the attitude within the organisation was when the CEO said 'Jump', people responded with

'How high?' An aggressive approach was seen as the one that worked around the organisation, based on the top leaders' behaviour.

Yet often CEOs confide during their coaching how isolated they feel, particularly from the truth of what is going on in their organisations. Here is the opportunity for them to explore their own behaviour and consider why that might be the case and what cultural forces, role modelled by themselves, are holding the lack of honest feedback in place. To be a leader in an organisation, particularly a senior one, is a conscious choice, born out of specific individual motivation. And coming with that are certain responsibilities.

Be responsible for yourself

This means developing your self- and social-awareness. A leader striving ultimately to satisfy their unconscious ego, fixed in their thinking to gain power, make money, look after themselves at the cost of others, is driven by their own survival needs. These can be so strong that the leader is too unwilling or fearful to take a look at themselves and the impact they have on those around them. This is not the sort of leader required in today's organisations.

What is required of leaders is to possess a level of consciousness around how they, their beliefs, values, emotions, experiences (self-awareness), and attitude and behaviour (social-awareness) affect others. Being responsible for that means setting aside your ego to do what is required for the greater good of the organisation and the people you lead. This is hard to do without understanding yourself and the impact you can have, and is certainly helped by creating clarity around your own purpose and vision and what you stand for as a contributor to your organisation and the world as a whole. It also means being a leader who is willing to open up to learning, feedback, self-understanding and insights, be vulnerable in the face of not knowing, and be willing to flex your attitude and behaviour.

Being responsible for yourself means holding yourself to account, checking in on your own integrity regularly. Knowing your integrity is intact gives you a sense of personal power, and makes it much easier to hold those around you to account too.

Create possibility from love, not fear

Leadership is about inspiring, engaging, getting the most from others, navigating towards a destination. A leader's job is to manage themselves and their emotions, keeping a balance between head and heart so that they can respond to whatever circumstances they face in a powerful way.

Power comes from not taking things personally, recognising our own vulnerabilities and triggers, and being able to manage these. When our egos are triggered, we jump into defensive reactions of attacking or retreating, both of which are fear based. What can really help us and those around us is to come from a place of compassion and love. This doesn't mean we become soft and mushy. Love can be fierce and strong, but coming from love means our intentions are positive and seeking the greater good rather than the survival and distrustful mentality that fear evokes.

Coming from love also means seeing the greater good in others. Suspend judgement and right and wrong; work with what is so and build from there. When you're exploring difference, be curious rather than judgemental to open up the space for difficult conversations to be much easier and support the creation of collaboration.

Engaging with a loving possibility helps you as a leader create a future that is emotionally compelling, and this in turn engages others and brings them on board. Leaders who are open to learn and consider what is possible and engage with the contribution of others are able to co-create a compelling vision that people are much more likely to commit to. This ensures high levels of ownership and alignment. Once a leader has a team aligned around a compelling vision, then the momentum of the team getting into action can become an unstoppable force.

In uncertain and complex times, having a vision as a statement of intent provides a powerful focus. And the key is that it is emotionally compelling and appealing, and owned and championed by the senior leadership team. A vision that is co-created by the senior team makes it even more compelling as each leader has had an input, fulfilling many ego needs around control and acknowledgement.

REALITY CHECK

In which Tom learns the power of co-creating a positive future with his team

Tom was a newly appointed MD, leading a service and sales business. He inherited an underperforming operation and a demand from the parent company for the business to move into profit.

Tom quickly identified the structure of his director team as being out of balance. Silo working predominated and the reputation of the team was one of a change-resistant group. Conscious of the pressure he was under, Tom restructured the team. This was met with agreement on the surface from the team, but inertia when it came to making the change happen.

I supported Tom to manage his directors' behaviour by having conversations with each one to understand their perspective and resistance. Tom saw that he had tried to make change without engaging his team, but stood by the need for this change to happen. He organised an off-site meeting which focused on relationship building, communication and creating a safe environment where people could speak openly. This developed a level of honesty, trust and alignment that had been missing before and the team co-created a vision and strategy they all owned which addressed the need for a turnaround in performance.

Three months on, the structural changes had been implemented and the team was working cohesively. Nine months on, the business had gone into profit. When asked what had made the difference, Tom commented that it was having some uncomfortable conversations during the off-site followed by the awareness of how powerful this was in creating openness and accountability.

Leave people in a better place

There are fundamental questions for leaders to consider. Firstly, have you left people more empowered and able than they were before? Consider how you engage as a leader with others, passing on leadership skills and encouraging them to grow and develop, so they too can step up. This occurs in the day-to-day business and interactions of an organisation when you give time, support and coaching, creating an environment of positive social communication which means everyone feels better at the end of each conversation.

Then ask yourself, 'How am I contributing to all of my stakeholders' success?' What is your view of each of your stakeholders? Are they there to help you, or you to help them? When you're seeking personal success, consider collective success. By contributing to all the people in your network being successful, you will find that you will be too.

Then ask yourself what you want to be remembered for. As a leader, what is the difference you want to make overall? Consider the legacy you want to leave behind, both in terms of visible changes and results, and in how people experienced you.

How do you engage people in the changes you want to make and give away the action and the glory so that others can shine? Part of this responsibility is to make yourself redundant, which means being able to delegate, let go of the detail and free yourself to be more strategic. How leaders embrace change and take responsibility is core to making any change happen.

Clearly stated outcomes, behaviours and competencies

So often, cultural change initiatives fail because of a lack of clarity around what is expected. We tend to change what can be measured, so a statement of intent is not enough. A framework of what the change looks like, so it can be measured and integrated into every element of an organisation's structure, makes what is often implicit explicit. Clear behavioural competencies provide understanding. Including them in performance measures and reviews makes them tangible expectations and a focus for feedback and development at all levels of the organisation.

Using an appreciative approach really helps here. Focusing on strengths reinforces what works and builds confidence and positive energy into the system.

Ongoing development over a period of time

Changing culture means changing behaviour. Whatever choice of development method you select, one-off, solitary approaches are a bit like popping an ice cube into a drink on a hot day. It will soon melt, so its impact is short term.

For sustainable change, development on a psychological and behavioural basis takes time. We are talking about shifting unconscious behaviours and habits often formed from long-standing beliefs designed to protect ourselves and our egos. Programmes of development I've seen work best are those that:

- Take place over a period of months

- Enable time to stand back to see what would otherwise not be seen

- Present clear benefits for leaders' own development

- Address blind spots

- Encourage people to be responsible for their learning

- Use everyday working situations for participants to apply their learning and practise new skills

- Are reinforced by a selection of activities in the workplace, eg recognition and reward when new behaviours are working

Time taken to connect and engage with people

Ticking a box to say you have completed a programme of change is different to actually engaging and being fully connected to it. Behavioural change requires taking an honest look at yourself and owning the development you want or need to make. How any development is set up, the messaging of it, the support from line managers and others in the workplace will make a massive difference to whether leaders fully engage.

Change often causes people's survival ego to kick in. This can be expressed in several ways:

- **Cynicism** – openly criticising and damning the whole process

- **Avoidance** – people keeping their heads down and being too busy to participate

- **Denial** – 'It's not me, it's someone else who needs to change'

On an organisational level, when you're creating a shift in culture, some people will not come on board. It will be a move too far away from their personal values, so you need to accept that there will be fallout. Part of navigating egos in service of cultural change is that those who do not come on board have a right and a choice to hold their view, and this will have an impact and consequence.

The important point here is to avoid a 'done to' approach for both those who have bought into the change and those who have resisted it. Some people will want to leave; others may not leave, but also won't buy in. Appealing to people's needs during this time is more important than ever to help you all come to a co-created conclusion. To capitalise on any development activity, provide a structure from which people can manage their own learning that supports them to be in charge of their development and responsible for the decisions and choices they make.

Accountability is built into the process

The culture changes I've observed that have worked most effectively are those that include honesty and the ability to give feedback and challenge when leaders' behaviour is contrary to the desired behaviour. This is when senior leaders' involvement is most important. It is not just the job of HR to oversee progress, but that of each and every line leader from the top of the organisation. If senior leaders are not holding their teams to account, and are similarly not being held to account by their leader, then the cultural drift will sweep in and there will be a return to the status quo.

REALITY CHECK

Where the leader got fully behind the culture change

Director Don was totally bought into the behaviours required in the new culture. He ensured that every member of his division participated in a programme of change that developed these behaviours, and his division transformed and provided a glowing example to the rest of the organisation around what was possible.

Another part of the organisation was led by Tony, a director who did not buy in and was not held accountable by his line. Some of Tony's people participated in the development programme. They were initially cynical and nervous about being there, but in the end engaged and took away valuable learning. Returning to their department, they were frustrated by the lack of engagement they experienced from their line and other senior managers in the division. Consequently, Tony's division did not change.

Summary

Changing culture is not easy because we are dealing with collective egos and blind spots in the form of cultural norms. But it is possible to create shifts in culture. How leaders engage, buy into and lead that change is at the heart of it being successful. Leaders taking responsibility for themselves and their impact can be the difference that creates a positive culture.

Don't expect a one-off or one-size-fits-all approach to make culture change happen. We are talking about something that is complex and we're not fully conscious of, so it benefits most from a variety of aligned activities.

REFLECTION

- How would you describe your organisation's collective ego?

- Stepping back, consider some of the cultural norms at play. Which ones support positive culture and which ones don't?

- To what extent do you embody the leadership responsibilities highlighted in this chapter?

- How is this reflected in your organisation?

- What conclusions are you drawing from this overall reflection?

Conclusion

As our journey together draws to a close, my hope is that you will have gained some valuable insights into how your ego can be activated, and how this is impacting you and those you come into contact with in your role as leader. With this increased understanding, you can take away strategies for managing your own ego drives and navigating the egos of those around you.

Dancing around the roles of victim, persecutor and rescuer is something we all do. These roles, along with our internal imposter, critic, competitor, child or parent, are all different manifestations of our ego. You may have learned that you have some manifestations that apply specifically to you, and that is OK. What it is important for you to accept is that there are many different elements to everyone's personality; this is what makes each of us unique.

Leading ourselves and others effectively does not mean losing our own uniqueness. What it means is honing certain elements through self-understanding and self-care, strengthening the parts that enable us to transcend our ego drives and come from a place of greater humanity and compassion for both ourselves and others. There are certain vital and inter-linked elements that enable us to get over our own egos and navigate our relationships with others:

- The ability to be present and in touch with the here and now, to notice ourselves and what is going on around us. What helps us develop this sense of alertness is a high level of self-care and attention to wellbeing, including practices such as meditation, connecting with nature or physical exercise. These practices allow us the chance to quieten our busy minds – a breeding ground for our ego traps.

- Being willing to commit time out to reflect on a regular basis. Even small amounts of time to review and learn inform us on so many levels and support our positive intentions on how to approach the situations we find challenging.

- Developing our sense of purpose and why we do what we do, be it on a big-picture level in terms of our life purpose or what we want to contribute in our current role and organisation. Purpose gives us meaning and an anchor we can connect to, which helps us manage our emotional state and our ego reactions.

- When we're caught in a moment where our ego is activated, the simplest thing to do is to take a breath. Not only does this provide oxygen to our brain, it also provides a pause, and that split second can make all the difference. If our ego reaction is just too strong, then it's OK to take time out. We can always request a pause in the proceedings and reconvene later.

As a leader in an organisation, you will have many demands put upon you and those you lead. These demands provide circumstances ripe for triggering egos. What is helpful is not to get into the 'drama'; instead, accept, learn and be different next time. A leader's job when leading change while faced with repetitive past-based patterns of behaviour is to choose something different. If you do this more often than not, then you have access to not only change, but also transformation. The key is to accept, learn, move on and apply what you have learned.

The journey to getting over yourself to lead begins with being honest about what is working or not working. Strengthening your ability to manage your ego drives and stay out of your own way will give you a greater sense of personal power, confidence and belief. Who knows what's round the corner? Whatever it is, if you can manage your ego, you will be ready, willing and able to meet the challenge.

References

Books

Berne, E (1964) *Games People Play: The psychology of human relationships*. USA: Random House

Blanchard, K, Burrows, H and Oncken, W (1990) *The One Minute Manager Meets The Monkey: Free up your time and deal with priorities.* London: Thorsons

Buckingham, M and Coffman, C (2005) *First, Break All The Rules: What the world's greatest managers do differently.* London: Simon & Schuster

Harris, TA (1973) *I'm OK – You're OK: Climb out of the cellar of your mind.* London: Random House

Johansen, R (2012) *Leaders Make The Future: Ten new leadership skills for an uncertain world.* San Francisco: Berrett-Koehler

Karpman, SB (2014) *A Game Free Life: The definitive book on the Drama Triangle and Compassion Triangle by the originator and author.* Drama Triangle Publications

Loehr, J and Schwartz, T (2005) *The Power Of Full Engagement: Managing energy, not time, is the key to high performance and personal renewal.* New York: The Free Press

Stuart, I and Joines, V (1993) *TA Today: A new introduction to transactional analysis.* Nottingham: Lifespace Publishing

Articles

Clance, P and Imes, S (1978) 'The Imposter Phenomenon in High Achieving Women: Dynamics and therapeutic intervention'. *Psychotherapy: Theory, Research and Practice,* Volume 15:3, Georgia State University

Gallup (2017) 'State Of The American Workplace'. www.gallup.com/workplace/238085/state-american-workplace-report-2017.aspx

Goleman, D (2000) 'Leadership That Gets Results'. *Harvard Business Review,* March – April, https://hbr.org/2000/03/leadership-that-gets-results

Films

The Corporation (2003), directed by Mark Achbar and Jennifer Abbot, written by Joel Bakan, Harold Crooks and Mark Achbar

Interview with David Bowie taken from the film *Inspirations* (1997) by Michael Apted, www.imdb.com/title/tt0125249

Acknowledgements

In writing this book, I have been on my own journey of getting over myself and my ego. I'd like to thank all the people who have supported and encouraged me along the way.

Orla Power, Penny De Valk, Jake Watkins, Jackie Lawlor, Deborah Seago and Samantha Culver for your valued review and feedback on my initial draft. Craig McMurrough, Elva Ainsworth, Niall O'Connor, Ed Garcez and Penny De Valk for your final read through and endorsements.

All members of my MasterMind group and WhatsApp writers' group, and the Book Midwife herself, Mindy Gibbons-Kline, for getting me on the road.

The team at Rethink Press for your integrity and support in the editing and referencing process, particularly Catriona Hoyle, Alison Jack and Verity Ridgman.

My friends, family, colleagues and clients for your positivity and enthusiasm, which have consistently inspired me and kept me going. Jonathan Banks, my partner, for your never-ending support and pragmatism. Thank you!

Finally, I wish to dedicate this book to my mother who passed away in 2019. She possessed quite an ego herself, but she learned to use that part of herself to do good in her community and family, despite growing up in an age where being strong and a leader was not necessarily encouraged in a woman.

The Author

Mary Gregory is a sought-after international leadership consultant. She has led change for organisations including First Choice Holidays, O2, Ralph Lauren and Tesco. A trusted coach to senior executives, she also designs and delivers large-scale leadership programmes.

Having learned through both her work and life how our ego can hold us back, Mary is committed to empowering leaders to create workplaces where people thrive. Integrating her experience from her career, which she began as a therapist in child and family psychiatry, with developing leaders and leading change in blue-chip organisations, Mary utilises her deep understanding of what makes humans and organisations tick to support her clients to enable sustainable change. The programmes she designs are lively and interactive, and put the organisation and learner at the centre of the experience. Her clients describe her as a warm, compassionate, challenging and tenacious coach who helps them achieve the results they want through expanding their thinking and taking a deeper look to access the insights and courage to take positive action. Formal training in personal and organisational psychology, coaching and facilitation gives her a strong psychological foundation to her work.

To connect with Mary:
- @MaryEGregory
- www.linkedin.com/in/marygregory
- www.marygregory.com
- mary@marygregory.com

Printed in Great Britain
by Amazon

44028109R00132